1987

# Human Sexuality
# in
# Medical Social Work

The *Journal of Social Work & Human Sexuality* series:

- Social Work and Child Sexual Abuse, edited by Jon R. Conte and David A. Shore
- *Human Sexuality in Medical Social Work,* edited by Larry Lister and David A. Shore
- *Homosexuality and Social Work,* edited by Robert Schoenberg and Richard Goldberg, with David A. Shore

# Human Sexuality in Medical Social Work

Larry Lister
David A. Shore
Co-Editors

The Haworth Press
New York

*Human Sexuality in Medical Social Work* has also been published as *Journal of Social Work & Human Sexuality,* Volume 2, Number 1, Fall 1983.

The Haworth Press, Inc., 28 East 22 Street, New York, NY 10010

**Library of Congress Cataloging in Publication Data**
Main entry under title:

Human sexuality in medical social work.

Also published as Journal of social work & human sexuality, v. 2, no. 1. fall 1983.
Includes bibliographies.
Contents: Direct social work practice, human sexuality, and health care systems / Larry Lister—A social work perspective on sexual health / Harvey L. Gochros—Addressing the sexual needs of patients in health care systems / David A. Shore, Janice M. Pyrce—[etc.]
1. Medical social work—Addresses, essays, lectures. 2. Sick—Sexual behavior—Addresses, essays, lectures. 3. Sex—Addresses, essays, lectures. I. Lister, Larry. II. Shore, David A. [DNLM: 1. Sex behavior. 2. Social work. W1 J0889D v.2, no. 11
HV687.H83 1984          362.1'0425          83-26449
ISBN 0-86656-254-0

# Human Sexuality
# in
# Medical Social Work

Journal of Social Work & Human Sexuality
Volume 2, Number 1

## CONTENTS

## About the Editors

Larry Lister is an Associate Professor at the University of Hawaii School of Social Work, where he is chair of the Direct Practice Concentration and Coordinator of Continuing Education. Dr. Lister is former director of Social Services at Leahi Hospital. He has written in the areas of health and human sexuality and currently he is developing material on a comprehensive approach to social work practice with families.

David A. Shore is the Associate Director, Accreditation Program for Psychiatric Facilities, Joint Commission on Accreditation of Hospitals, and the founding editor of the *Journal of Social Work & Human Sexuality*. Certified by the American Association of Sex Educators, Counselors and Therapists in all three categories, Mr. Shore provides consultation and staff development programs for health and social service agencies, and schools and residential facilities throughout the United States and abroad. He serves on editorial boards of social work and sexology journals in the United States, England and Japan and has published numerous articles, monographs and books. Mr. Shore is the recipient of four consecutive grants from the Playboy Foundation to study various aspects of human sexuality.

# Contributors

**Trudy Darty,** BS, Independent Researcher, Harrisonburg, Virginia.

**Harvey Gochros,** DSW, School of Social Work, University of Hawaii, Honolulu, Hawaii.

**James Gripton,** DSW, Faculty of Social Welfare, University of Calgary, Calgary, Alberta, Canada.

**Thomas R. Jones,** LCSW, Psychiatric Social Worker, Camarillo State Hospital, Camarillo, California.

**Constance Lindemann,** Dr PH, School of Social Work, The University of Oklahoma, Norman, Oklahoma.

**Larry Lister,** DSW, School of Social Work, University of Hawaii, Honolulu, Hawaii.

**Sandra J. Potter,** PhD, James Madison University, Harrisonburg, Virginia.

**Janice M. Pyrce,** ACSW, Manager, Community Relations, *Hospital Corporation* of *America Psychiatric Company,* Forest Park, Illinois.

**Mary S. Sheridan,** ACSW, Social Worker, Pulmonary Service, Kapiolani/Children's Medical Center, Honolulu, Hawaii.

**David A. Shore,** ACSW, Associate Director, Accreditation Program for Psychiatric Facilities, Joint Commission on Accreditation of Hospitals, Chicago, Illinois, and Editor, *Journal of Social Work & Human Sexuality.*

**Mary Valentich,** PhD, Faculty of Social Welfare, University of Calgary, Calgary, Alberta, Canada.

For Connie Lister, with all my love

&

For Charlotte Shore, as we embark upon our life together
And for Trudy Darty, whose message in this book goes well beyond
her professional concern and represents, as well, her great courage.

# Preface

An entire text devoted to human sexuality in medical social work? This would seem to carry a concept of specialization to its outer limit, since it was not all that many years ago that all of social work was encompassed in one or two basic texts.

We hope, however, that a careful reading of this book will show that several themes are being dealt with simultaneously. First, we are offering a conceptualization of direct social work practice which encompasses a number of roles for the social worker in health care systems. The potential impact of social workers in health care settings (we are aware of the limitations inherent in our use of Medical Social Work in our title) is much greater than patient assessment in out-patient clinics and discharge planning in hospitals. We hope some of the diversity of roles which social workers can assume will itself offer a broadened perspective on social work practice in health care.

Secondly, we envision social work in health care as representing not only the diversity of ways in which the social worker may impact on clients and service systems, but we see health care as increasingly the concern of all social workers, not only those who work in "medical" settings. As a result, some of the content of this text is relevant to specific health settings, but much of it crosses service systems and is relevant to our work with clients wherever we may encounter them.

Finally, what is sexuality? If we take a narrow view that it represents sexual behavior, then we become forced into models of intervention which tend to focus on "plumbing" problems, to use Gochros' colorful terminology. We envision the domains (or "spheres") of sexuality as representing a diversity of concerns, so that when we consider how we may make an impact on behalf of patients' sexuality, we have a wide domain of possibilities to consider—some clinical, some interpersonal, some organizational, some structural.

In order to explore the various perspectives we have outlined above, we have organized the work to first provide some discussion of the model outlined above (Lister) and some perspective on what is sexual health (Gochros). As can be seen by Gochros' discussion, such a consideraton is a value and attitude issue, more than a biophysical one. We then offer several chapters related to the themes of social work intervention at the system development and maintenance levels (Shore and Pyrce) and for purposes of system linkage (Lister). A chapter is then devoted to assessment (Gripton and Valentich) when the focus is on the client with physical health problems. The remainder of the book presents a number of significant health problems (Darty and Potter on cancer; Sheridan on chronic illness), patient characteristics (Jones on dual diagnosis patients) and issues (Lindemann on menopause), each of which illustrates various sexual issues and the varieties of social work intervention responses which may be possible.

While the above seem to be neat categories for placing each of the contributions to this volume, their neatness also constrains and limits the range of material which is actually contained in each chapter. The chapter by Darty and Potter, as an important case in point, is written as much to focus on women's experiences in receipt of health care as it is to clarify the cancer experience. Thus the very point of this volume is thereby illustrated in this one example: we need a breadth of view when considering social work practice with sexual issues in health care.

So, to answer our opening question, we feel there is ample justification—based on the content presented—for an entire text devoted to considerations of sexuality by social workers in health care systems. Especially since sexual issues can so easily be overlooked by any of the other health care providers, it seems that we social workers have an area of service open which, if not filled by us, may simply constitute a gap in total health care. We hope this volume may serve as a resource for social workers to use in helping bridge any gap which may otherwise exist between people and the services which should exist to meet their needs as fully as possible.

*Larry Lister*
*David A. Shore*

# Human Sexuality
# in
# Medical Social Work

# Direct Social Work Practice, Human Sexuality, and Health Care Systems

Larry Lister, DSW

Social work in health care systems has the potential for making a major contribution to identifying and providing for the sex-related needs of consumers. While increasingly much is written in social work about sexuality, nowhere has there been a reference source devoted solely to the subject of sexuality and health care systems. Most schools of social work offer courses on sexuality, but available information indicates that the integration of this content throughout other courses in the curriculum is limited (Mazer and Kunkel, 1979). Since sexual issues could be considered when discussing nearly any aspect of health and illness (i.e., see the articles in the last section of this publication), it is timely to highlight the interaction of issues of sexuality, health, and social work practice and to explore some of the ways in which social workers can incorporate this perspective in their practice.

The purpose of this introductory chapter is to look at the issues of sexuality, health systems, and social work direct practice in order to identify a relevant perspective within which the other contributions to this volume may be viewed. While the three components of sexuality, health systems, and clusters of social work roles will be dealt with separately, it is hoped the reader will see these as a system which, when functioning in an integrated manner, offers a potential for impacting at multiple levels, at various times, and with diverse means of intervention.

## DEFINITIONS OF SEXUALITY

When referring to sexuality, at least four "spheres" of human experience may be identified (Lister, 1981). These spheres may be identified as: (1) the biological and reproductive, including the nature and processes of reproduction and the various ways in which genetic influences, diseases or other pathological processes may alter physiology or may influence the other spheres; (2) gender identity and sex role behavior. In this sphere, an individual's inner sense of his/her genetic endowment as either a male or female interacts with society's expectations for what is considered masculine and feminine, and which influences; (3) sex activity, as this is expressed privately or in interaction with other persons or objects, and finally; (4) the influence of erotic and sensual stimuli, as these are experienced internally (both sensorially and cognitively) by each individual.

To illustrate the above perspectives, a social worker might be concerned with developing and delivering a sex-education program as part of a family planning series on conception (sphere 1), or the focus may be on revising policies in a health care setting which have been found to be sexist (sphere 2), or intervention may be involved with helping a man with irreversible impotence find other ways of sexually satisfying his partner (item 3), or helping staff in a rehabilitation facility to appreciate the need for continued sensual experience by paralyzed patients (the fourth sphere).

## HEALTH CARE SETTINGS

As implied above, social workers may influence health from within or outside of a wide range of practice settings. Indeed, the social worker need not be identified as a "medical" social worker in order to focus on the health of clients. We are increasingly aware of the central position which health plays in influencing all aspects of people's lives, so that social workers in all settings need to make the assessment of clients' health an integral part of total care.

Table 1 illustrates several of the key components which must be taken into consideration when defining health settings or related systems. As can be seen, three broad categories are designated: residential, community, and other, the latter representing the many other settings of social work practice where social workers may influence health, even though the setting is not created for that purpose (i.e., community centers, family service agencies, correctional institutions). A listing of all the types of residential and community health facilities is not provided here; however such a list would require, in only the residential category, for example, a progression

Table 1

A Model for the

Categorization of Health Settings

| Types of Settings (examples) | Populations Served (examples) | |
|---|---|---|
| | By Demographics | By Diagnoses |
| **Residential/In-Patient Health Care** | | |
| Acute/Short-Term | children | orthopedic |
| Long-Term/Hospice | private patients | cancer |
| **Community/Out-Patient Health Care** | | |
| Out-Patient Clinic | public assistance receipients | acute illness |
| State Health Department | state residents | communicable diseases |
| **Other Settings** * | | |

* The category for Other Settings is necessary in order to indicate that prevention and maintenance programs related to health are increasingly the domain of other community systems.

from the most temporary acute-care in-patient setting (such as would be required for a laparoscopy) to long-term and terminal care facilities. In the same manner, the community settings could be categorized according to at least two dimensions: (1) the complexity of services (for example, a simple dispensary as contrasted with a multi-purpose state health department) or (2) according to the variety of issues dealt with (i.e., an arthritis foundation as contrasted with a university research center).

It is suggested in the table that two of the major means for further distinguishing differences in either residential or community health settings/systems are: (1) demographics and (2) diagnoses. Thus, as shown in the table, an acute hospital may admit only children or may be organized for orthopedic health problems, while a community clinic may serve only the indigent or may provide only emergency services for acute problems. Whatever the categories, the point is that, in the same manner that the term sexuality needs elaboration, health systems are not uni-dimensional and their diversity will influence both the clusters of status-roles which social workers may select and the types of sex issues which may need to be addressed.

## CLUSTERS OF SOCIAL WORKER STATUS-ROLES

As shown in Table 2, there are four status-role clusters, each of which relates to various goals which are appropriate for social workers to carry out in delivering health care services. The clusters progress from the more "macro" level of developmental activities to the "micro," or clinical, level. The clusters also represent social work in the aggregate in health care, rather than roles which would be performed by every social worker. Thus, the clusters should be viewed in system's terms as an arrangement of parts which, in their totality, function to deliver social work services to persons involved in the health service complex. Each cluster can be described in terms of (1) goals which are directed to defined (2) focal or change systems and which require diverse (3) social worker statuses and role activities which utilize various (4) techniques, skills or processes.

### System Development

The first cluster is termed System Development. As implied in the title, the goals of this cluster of statuses and roles are to create health care systems which are basically pro-people; that is, designed so that health promotion and care are compatible with the needs and diversity of the population served. This cluster represents social work direct practice at the broadest level, since it has as its focal systems the organizations which deliver health services, rather than its focus being on specific individuals. Thus, the setting up of exam-

Table 2

Clusters of Social Work Status-Roles

I. System Development
    Goals: develop health services
    Focal systems: health services
    Status-roles:                          Skills, processes, techniques[*]
        1. Policy and procedure developer    _____
        2. Planner    _____
        3. Researcher    _____

II. System Maintenance
    Goals: maintain and enhance health services
    Focal systems: social workers and other personnel within a health system
    Status-roles:                          Skills, processes, techniques[*]
        1. Administrator/manager    _____
        2. Consultant    _____
        3. Supervisor    _____
        4. Teacher/in-service trainer    _____

III. System Linkage
    Goals: connect consumers/patients with resources
    Focal systems: patient/consumers and resources
    Status-roles:                          Skills, processes, techniques[*]
        1. Case manager/coordinator    _____
        2. Broker    _____
        3. Mediator/negotiator    _____
        4. Advocate    _____

IV. Clinical
    Goals: provide therapeutic services
    Focal systems: patients/consumers
    Status-roles:                          Skills, processes, techniques[*]
        1. Caseworker/therapist    _____
        2. Family therapist    _____
        3. Group worker/therapist    _____

---

[*] The skills, processes and techniques are used to implement each of the status-roles and are not spelled-out here but are illustrated in various chapters in this book.

ination rooms at a family planning clinic in order to assure reasonable privacy would be an example of how the development of the service system can be the focus for planning from a social work perspective.

In order to accomplish the developmental goals specific for this cluster, three professional social statuses have been identified. Statuses, or positions in a social structure, are defined in terms of the behaviors (roles) which a person carries out, roles which are based on social expectations (Lister, 1982).

The three statuses which have been assigned to the development cluster are: *planner, policy/procedure developer,* and *researcher.* Singly, or in combination, these are the primary statuses which may be assumed by social workers when participating in the development of health services.

It is recognized that the developmental status-roles may be carried out at various levels of society (local to national) an in relation to widely diverse issues (i.e., federal social welfare policy vs. a new service component in a community health system). This paper is concerned with the implementation of these status-roles at the direct practice level of social work, when that level of practice is conceptualized in broader terms than what is historically thought of as casework (Sanders et al., 1982).

There is diversity of opinion about what are the behaviors (roles) which are relevant to each of the statuses listed in this cluster. Indeed, many authors omit any discussion of roles and instead focus on the tasks and processes necessary for developmental work and on the varied contextual factors which influence the developmental process. For example, in a discussion of practitioner roles associated with the statuses of planner and community organizer, Rothman summarized the opinions of several writers as follows:

> Grosser has portrayed the enabler, broker, advocate, and activist in neighborhood work; Sanders uses the analyst, planner, organizer and program administrator in overseas community development; Ross—for all settings—uses the guide, enabler, expert, and social therapist. Most recently, roles in planning for delinquency control were described by Spergel as enabler, advocate, organizer and developer. (Rothman, note 1)

In a discussion of advocacy planning, Davidoff states: "The advocate planner would be more than a provider of information, an analyst of current trends, a simulator of future conditions, and a detailer of means. In addition to carrying out these necessary parts of planning, he would be a proponent of specific substantive solutions" (Davidoff, note 2).

It should be pointed out, also, that the researcher status in the System Development cluster refers to survey, community needs assessment and other such research methods which help to identify the direction new services might take, rather than evaluative research which helps monitor progress or assess outcomes of services. This latter type of evaluation would be a component of all three of the other role clusters presented in Table 2.

As can be seen in the foregoing discussion, status-roles overlap extensively in social work. However, at the wider level, the roles specified in this cluster are all directed to system development.

The final component in the present model of status-role clusters is concerned with the actual techniques, processes and skills which the social worker uses to perform the role activity required of each status. Since social work practice is based on a process which involves data-gathering, assessment, intervention and evaluation, there are a fundamental set of activities which are involved in implementing the status-roles in all four clusters. However, the specific skills, techniques and processes utilized for research are different from those which are required for clinical interventions and because of their complexity they cannot be listed here, but are elaborated in some of the chapters which follow.

## System Maintenance

The next cluster of status-roles is termed system maintenance, with the goals concerned with maintaining, perpetuating, and enhancing systems once they have been developed. In other words, not only is it important to create desirable systems, but they need to be maintained in order for them to remain dynamic and responsive to the needs of consumers. Thus, a cluster of roles are directed toward the internal, intraorganizational workings of health systems, the goals of which are to continually modify or strengthen existing services.

The statuses identified in this cluster are: administrator/manager, consultant, supervisor, teacher (including in-service trainer) and team member. Each of these statuses require role activities directed toward other members of the health system, rather than direct interaction with patients. Some of these status-roles (i.e., supervisor) are more intra-professionally focused; that is, they require skills and functions which are directed to other social workers, while other of these status-roles are more inter-disciplinary in focus (team member) and require interactions of the social worker with other disciplines in the health complex. In addition, these roles are mainly carried out within an organization (i.e., supervisor), but several of them may be used to help maintain outside organizations (i.e., consultant).

In order to implement the roles expected in each of the above statuses, many skills are required of the social worker. As only one example, attitudes and expectations about patients and their sexuality may differ greatly from one professional group to another. Consequently, if the social worker is supervising another social worker, the base-line knowledge and attitudes which are shared in common may call for different role behavior than when that same social worker is acting as a team member with professionals with quite different perspectives. The chapter by Gochros and some of the examples in the chapter by Lister elaborate on this theme: the chapter by Shore and Pyrce gives some further information concerning various of the maintenance roles and some of the complexity involved in social work intervention at this system maintenance level.

### System Linkage

The third cluster of status-roles has as its focal system the patient-families and their interactions with various resources. In this cluster, the goals are to help consumers connect with the resources needed to maintain and enhance health, in its broadest sense. The status-roles in this cluster are the traditional ones utilized by social work when concerned with the "situation" in the person-in-situation configuration; those *professional* roles which social workers use to help clients carry out their own desired *personal* roles (Lister, 1982). The four status-roles listed for this cluster are: case manager/coordinator, broker, mediator/negotiator, and advocate. As can be seen by the statuses identified, the goals consist of creating a linkage of clients and systems. Some of the processes involved in the implementation of these roles require minimal effort (i.e., a simple referral of a client), while others require complex activites (case management). Since this cluster is discussed more fully in the later chapter, it will not be further developed here (see Lister chapter).

### Clinical

There are many ways to title this cluster, but since all the skills required are appropriate to therapeutic work at the direct practice level, the cluster is referred to as clinical. The goals for all role activity in this cluster are to implement the basic social work process through direct contacts with patients. This cluster cannot be implemented in health systems out of the context of each of the above clusters, however, so it must be seen as part of a total configuration which contributes to the overall impact of social work on health systems.

In the clinical cluster are the following status-roles: caseworker/therapist with individuals and couples, family therapist, and group worker/therapist. Each of these statuses requires complex role activities and almost unlimited permutations of tasks, skills and processes in order to accomplish clinical objectives. The very purpose of listing this cluster last aside from the logic of the progression from the more "macro" to the "micro" levels of social work intervention is to indicate by the simplicity of stating "caseworker," how detailed and involved are the activities of each one of the status-roles in the other three clusters. Because there is such a vast literature in social work explicating the roles of the caseworker, all the more should social work give attention to the complexities of the other status-roles and how they may impact on various life systems.

This fourth cluster is not intended to suggest that social work intervention at the clinical level is only focused on sexual dysfunctioning. Rather, clinical roles are important to issues in all of the "spheres" of sexuality as defined at the beginning of this paper and as illustrated in the several clinically-oriented papers in this book. Ultimately, it is what makes it social work, rather than any of the other health professions, that our concepts of clinical intervention reach well beyond restoration of impaired sexual performance.

## SUMMARY

This paper has presented a discussion of various ways in which the concept of "sexuality" may be defined, a consideration of some of the variety of systems which need to be considered when referring to health services, and, finally, a discussion of four clusters of status-roles which social workers use in order to impact on health and health care. Each of the chapters in this publication will present information of relevance to one or more of these subject areas and will demonstrate how rich and varied are the opportunities for the direct practice social worker to impact on issues of human sexuality.

## REFERENCE NOTES

1. Rothman, J. *Planning and Organizing for Social Change, Action Principles from Social Science Research.* New York: Columbia University Press, 1974, p. 36.
2. Davidoff, P. Advocacy and Pluralism in Planning. In N. Gilbert, H. Specht (Eds) *Planning for Social Welfare, Issues, Models and Tasks.* Englewood Cliffs, New Jersey: Prentice-Hall, 1977; p. 195.

## REFERENCES

Davidoff, P. Advocacy and Pluralism in Planning. In N. Gilbert and H. Specht, (Eds) *Planning for Social Welfare: Issues, Models and Tasks.* Englewood Cliffs, New Jersey: Prentice-Hall, 1977.

Lister, L. Chronically Ill and Disabled. In D. Shore and H. Gochros, *Sexual Problems of Adolescents in Institutions.* Springfield Illinois: Charles C. Thomas, 1981.

Lister, L. Role Training for Interdisciplinary Health Teams. *Health and Social Work,* 1982, 7, 19-25.

Mazer, C. & Kunkel, D., Sex Education in Social Work: Present Status and Future Trends, in D. Kunkel (Ed.) *Sexual Issues in Social Work: Emerging Concerns in Education and Practice.* Honolulu, Hawaii: University of Hawaii School of Social Work, 1979.

Rothman, J. *Planning and Organizing for Social Change, Action Principles from Social Science Research.* New York: Columbia University Press, 1974.

Sanders, D., Kurren, O. & Fischer, J., (Eds) *Fundamentals of Social Work Practice, A Book of Readings.* Belmont, California: Wadsworth Publishing Company, 1982.

# A Social Work Perspective on Sexual Health

## Harvey L. Gochros, DSW

A discussion of sexual health* necessarily revolves around the exploration of sexual attitudes. That which is healthy is that which people—at least those people who have influence over many others—*consider* to be healthy. Many observers of human nature, from Aristotle to Albert Ellis, have correctly observed that it is not what happens to us, or even specifically what we do that matters. What does matter is how we perceive the activity. Nowhere is this more true than in the arena of human sexuality. Our attitudes and beliefs about what we do and what happens to us determines the effect of these events on us—and our sexual well-being. A corollary of this observation was noted by W.I. Thomas, "if something is perceived as real, then *it* is real in its consequences" (W.I. Thomas, *Social Behavior and Personality.* New York: Social Science Research Council, 1951, p. 81).

For example, two married men of the same age and general characteristics experience erectile difficulties with their wives. One might continue to caress and enjoy his intimate contact with his wife and ultimately drift off into sleep feeling okay about himself and his wife, feeling "sometimes it happens, and sometimes it doesn't." The other man tries and tries, and encourages his wife to try and try. The more they try the more he feels incompetent, sick, unmanly and worthless. He labels himself as "impotent" and sinks into depression.

The same situation, different attitudes and different results.

---

*The author has reluctantly used the term "sexual health" in both the title and content of this paper. The concept of "health" depends on a complementary concept of disease. Because I believe the concept of disease has no place in a discussion of human behavior (a belief extensively discussed by many other writers elsewhere), I would prefer to use other terms, such as satisfying, fulfilling, or functional. Such terms imply more than the absence of inferred "diseases." However, "health" has a positive sound to it and is the generally accepted term. So be it.

This paper will examine attitudes about sexual health, how they are formed and how they influence the sexual expression of various populations.

## FACTORS DETERMINING ATTITUDES ABOUT SEXUAL HEALTH

Sexual attitudes vary from person to person and from time to time. A number of factors tend to shape them. No person, client, professional helper, or "sex expert" is immune from these influences.

Take, for example, the present writer. There are several demographics about him which could *conceivably* affect what he chooses to say about sexual health. Out of the myriad of influences on him, let's examine five.

1) The writer is of Northern European ancestry. Thus, he is a member of the dominant ethnic group in America. His ethnic heritage is, Judeo-Christian, and he shares the puritan, Calvinistic heritage that still has a profound effect on the majority of white Americans.

2) The writer is male. He has never been pregnant, nor has he ever borne a child or nursed one. As a male he is bigger and stronger—less physically vulnerable—than most females. He has never been physically or emotionally overwhelmed by a partner, nor has he worried about it. He has been taught to be an assertive initiator of *contacts with other people*—including sexual contacts.

3) The writer is middle-aged. Middle-aged people have experienced physical and emotional changes over the years. For example, although orgasms are still a component of the sexual response of people regardless of age, as an individual gets older the orgasm becomes relatively less significant to the total sexual experience. Older people—especially older men—tend to get more romantic and less passionate. They also tend to deal more with their mortality and approach life and even sex more philosophically.

4) The writer is well-educated. He's got all the degrees through DSW. Indeed, he's even been employed for a generation as a university educator. Well-educated people tend to talk a great deal about human relationships. This includes sex. "What does it all mean?" "What is the nature of relationships" "Do we have a con-

tract?'' ''Let's examine our evolving sex-roles stereo-typing.'' Nothing is simple for the well-educated, certainly not sex.

5) The writer is employed, with a good income. He has job security, good medical care, good nutrition, privacy and considerable time for leisure. When our basic human needs are met, we go on to examine what else we can worry about. Sex, love, and commitment provide an outlet of concern, attention, even preoccupation for people who have almost everything else.

There are certainly many other variables which have contributed to the writer's sexual attitudes—religion, health, experiences, etc. These factors can lead to the development of an elaborate conceptual framework for sex which could be quite alien to many who are not of similar background. Indeed, the perception of this approach to sex may be analogous to watching a couple at the next table at McDonalds carefully laying out a linen tablecloth over their table, set it with fine china and crystal, pour some good wine, and leisurely sit back to savor their Big Mac.

Now it really doesn't matter all that much that the author of this treatise is a white, middle-aged, well-educated, and relatively affluent man. After all, this is only one chapter of one book. What *does* matter is that virtually everyone who has power over other peoples' sexual choices: judges, law makers, ministers, psychiatrists, sex experts, and television producers are *also* white, middle-aged, well-educated, and relatively affluent men. It is true that an occasional white, middle-aged, well-educated, and relatively affluent woman slips in and influences sexual activities, but that's still an exception, and often she has been coopted by the male world. The power of this powerful population in controlling everyone's sexuality through their possible biases must be taken into account when reviewing prevailing models for ''sexual health.''

## *PROFESSIONAL BIASES AND PERSPECTIVES*

Age, ethnicity, gender, education, and income are not the only influences on those who are sexual influencers. A ''sex expert's'' professional background may also determine the direction and emphasis of his or her sexual world view.

Perhaps the two most influential sexual scientists in the last century have been Alfred Kinsey and William H. Masters, both middle-aged, white males who were well-educated and financially comfortable. We have already discussed how these attributes can affect their perspectives: both what they chose to study, and how they went about interpreting what they found. In addition to these demographics, however, they also brought to their work their own professional biases. Kinsey was a biologist by training and philosophy. Thus, when he attempted to fill the void of knowledge about human sexuality, he approached it in the same way he would approach the understanding of any other kind of biological phenomenon: he measured and counted. How many people of what kind did, or started to do, a particular activity at what particular point in their lives. For a generation, this emphasis on numbers permeated both the professional and public view of sex.

Since many people tend to be vulnerable to outside influence and are looking for direction and limits to their sexual energies and interests, Kinsey's quantitative data seemed to offer some answers. "Normalcy" now had, or seemed to have, some empirical parameters.

A generation later, another white, middle-aged, well-educated, affluent man had an equally profound impact on American society. He, too, was influenced by a professional bias. William H. Masters is a gynecologist-physician. He saw the functioning of the human body, and particularly the sex organs, as the focus for his understanding of human sexuality. He studied and charted the physiological sexual responses and treated sexual "inadequacies." How the body worked was what was important, and almost exclusively in the context of heterosexual intercourse (with subsequent excursions into homosexual physical behavior). His work bred a generation of professional helpers well versed in the sexual response cycle and the mechanics of sexual intercourse, some of them even distorting the work of Master's and Johnson by becoming nothing more than sexual "plumbers."

## A Social Work Perspective

We have surveyed the professional biases of biology and medicine. Now lets consider social work's perspective on human sexuality. (Note that they have biases, while we have a perspective!)

I would suggest that looking at sex as a question of frequencies, or as a matter of enhanced physical functioning limits and distorts a comprehensive view of sexual functioning within its social context. It is this interplay of individual needs, wishes and desires with the support, demands, prohibitions and expectations of the social environment which provides a beginning understanding of sexual "health." That is, an individual who comfortably finds non-exploitive satisfaction of his or her sexual wishes and needs within the context of his or her social constellation has achieved sexual "health" or more accurately sexual functioning. It is the task of social workers to understand this complex interplay and to be prepared to intervene with social work skills to change or enhance both individual and social patterns which bring about sexual dysfunctioning. This may involve the gamut of social work services including counseling, education, policy changes, community reorganization and advocacy.

However, before we can charge into the quagmire of social work practice with sexual concerns, we had better return to some basic questions: What limits needs to be put on individual sexual expression? What is, or should be, the nature of appropriate social control of individual sexual behavior? How do we balance individual rights vs. the greater public good? Is everything all right?

To begin to answer these questions, we must first examine the sources of our current criteria for social control, consider how they are exercised and to what end. It is the compliance with social control of sexual expression which, to a large extent, defines sexual health.

## THE SOCIAL CONTROL OF SEXUAL EXPRESSION

Until fairly recently, there was an amazing degree of consensus about sexual "health" among the major social institutions which control sexual expression. Religions defined was what sexually acceptable as "moral" and what was unacceptable as "sinful." The law defined good sex as "legal" and the bad sex as "criminal." The mental health profession (currently the major locus of social control of sexual expression) has DSM-III full of control words: mentally healthy if it's acceptable and "deviation," "perversion," "fetish," "dysfunction," and, of course, "abnormal" if it's not. The attic of psychiatric terminology is full of labels still occasionally used to described unacceptable sexual states including such vague perjoratives as "frigid," "homosexual," "nymphomaniac," and "impotent." Such terms have been correctly referred to as more insults than diagnoses.

Surprisingly there is a common thread that historically connnects all these disparate institutions in their attempts to control sexual expression. The next section will describe the principle which underlies our basic concepts of "acceptable" sex, and to a significant degree defines what is sexual health.

## The Reproductive Bias

Until relatively recently, the strength of most nations, communities, religions, groups, and families could be measured by how many of the "right kind" of children were born into that nation, religion, community, group, or family and how well they were cared for. Each of these populations developed a concept of who ideal parents were and a set of concepts of the ideal situation in which those children might be raised. One thing was clear: sex should be channelized to positive reproductive ends.

Since these concepts of sex and reproduction were basic to the survival of the families, groups, communities, religions, and nations, various means of social control were developed to limit and focus sexual expression to those people and those activities which approximated the reproductive goals of that population. These values were subtly, and not so subtly, communicated to potentially sexually active individuals through such social institutions as the family, law, religion, the helping professions, folklore, and the media. Their social control messages can be defined as the "reproductive bias" which emphasized that:

"the only good, normal Christian, healthy, socially acceptable, legal, moral, beautiful sexual acts are those which could conceivably (pun intended) lead to a socially approved pregnancy."

Conversely, the more remote a person's behavior is from that which is associated with a socially approved pregnancy, the more likely she or he will be ridiculed, legislated against, or otherwise punished.

This bias not only defines the characteristics of people who can have sex, but also delimits the form of acceptable activities; thus, the poor, aged, disabled, homosexually oriented, members of ethnic minorities, the young, the old, and many others are either overlooked as sexual beings or have their sexuality suppressed, and activities other than coitus considered either unacceptable or just "foreplay."

Those whose sexual behavior could conceivably lead to a socially approved pregnancy usually represent the most powerful segments of our society: heterosexual, married, white, rich, intelligent, pre-golden-age adults. Most social institutions see these people and only these people as the sexual "elite," or those who are legitimately sexual.

A number of years ago, I described the sexual elite in the following slightly overstated way:

> The sexual elite is best exemplified by the idealized hero and heroine of the film *Love Story.* In that film, the hero is a young and handsome law student and the heroine is a young and beautiful music student. They fall in love immediately, engage in premarital intercourse—primarily as an expression of their love—and subsequently marry. She uses four letter words, but, underneath it all, is a "nice girl" who would not dream of marital infidelity. They have a great deal of fun and never stop loving each other until she dies an elegant death. Neither seems to feel love or affection for anyone else except for her father, who is sweet but passive. One is led to speculate that the hero is always potent, the heroine always achieves multiple sequential orgasms, and that they never need Kleenex. They seem to consider genital to genital intercourse in the missionary position culminating in simultaneous orgasm the logical and normal conclusion to every sexual activity that occurs 2.7 times a week immediately following Johnny Carson. This is obviously a stereotype of the sexual elite that is maintained by the white middle class. There are, of course, sexual stereotypes for every other American subculture. The ideal sexual model varies from group to group, place to place, and time to time. (Reference: Gochros, H.L. and Gochros, J.S., *The Sexually Oppressed,* New York: Association Press, 1977, pp. xx-xxi

It should be noted that the sexual elite may also suffer from the effects of the reproductive bias. The sexual elite must focus on intercourse (the most effective vehicle for reproduction). Women must seek an appropriate willing male to mate with in a committed relationship. Men must be willing and able to initiate intercourse, achieve and maintain erection and ejaculate at the right time and in the right place. Neither should get caught up in non-potentially-reproductive sexual interest such as self-stimulation or same-sex activities. Sex outside of marriage (either before or in addition to) is frowned upon since the sexual acts associated with such liaisons could not lead to socially approved pregnancy.

How are these norms of "health" (read: compatible with the reproductive bias) sex communicated? To a certain extent, these norms are communicated through such social institutions as the church, law, and the "helping" professions; but they are also communicated through folklore, the family, and peer groups. Fear of ridicule from friends (especially during the attitude-forming adolescent years), and modeling after socially accepted individuals shapes "healthy" behavior. For example, dirty jokes told by all age groups tend to convey messages about exactly what is expected in sexual behavior and what is unacceptable behavior, since it will be laughed at.

Another subtle vehicle of sexual social control of sexual "health" is language. For example, the activities we take for granted in everyday life tend to have short names: we talk, walk, eat, sleep, and laugh. Yet the terms for sexual activities have very different sounding names: we masturbate and engage in fellatio and cunnilingus. These words do not fit with "talk," "walk," "eat," "sleep," and "laugh"; they belong with "mononucleosis," "spinal meningitis," and "herpes simplex II." It is no accident that the words for many sexual activities—chief among them, masturbation—were invented to describe pathology and diseases. Masturbation for example, was manufactured from two root words, which, put together, mean "to rape or defile oneself by hand." Thus these words carry over an intended connotation of pathology.

The major alternatives to these pathological, antiseptic medical words are the common four letters words (most with abrasive "k" sounds in them) which put sex in the gutter. Thus our reproductive bias still gives us words for non-socially approved, non-reproductive sexual activities which are either pathological, dirty, or both.

Of course, the reproductive bias has begun to subside. The women's movement, the gay movement, and the growing recognition and acceptance of the sexual needs of such largely non-reproductive groups as the aged, the mentally retarded, and the disabled all reflect the breakdown of the bias.

However, a concept which has been supported by major social institutions and guided thousands of years of human sexual behavior dies hard. We still talk of the "reproductive organs" and "genitals." Our sex education of children invariably begins with an exposition on "where babies come from" as if that were the core of all sexual behavior. We still consider intercourse as the normal, natural aim of all sexual encounters (even the benign sounding concept of "foreplay" supports this bias: intercourse is "it"; other activities are just preliminaries.) We still consider homosexuality as "second best" at best and masturbation as perverse. We still think of sex as being legitimate for only physically and mentally healthy adult heterosexual, bonded couples. All these "preferences" stem from our reluctance to separate sex from reproduction. The reproductive bias still exerts a powerful control over our perceptions of acceptable, "healthy" sexuality.

However, it is the author's contention that any concepts of healthy sex must go beyond an evaluation of reproductive consequences. Sexual behavior cannot be evaluated outside of the context of its meaning for the individual and its relationship to other aspects of the individual's life. The state of health of a person's sexuality is an extension of what that person *wants* from his or her sexual activities. To the extent that these "wants" are achievable and do not exploit or harm others, they become the criteria for that person's sexual "health." Any other "standard" for health runs the risk of introducing personal, religious or other biases which have little place in our approach to helping people achieve their own legitimate life goals.

In helping people assess their sexual goals it may be useful, however, to explore what they might be expecting from their sexual activities. Sex is such a powerful phenomenon that it is frequently used as a tool to attempt to achieve non-sex related purposes. For example, some people use sex to avoid boredom, to gain acceptance, to achieve power, to barter, to humiliate, to reward or to punish.

A common use of sex is the attempt to achieve intimacy and assuage loneliness. This can be a futile pursuit. It reflects our transient society's paucity of vehicles for intimacy. Indeed, our weak provision for intimacy needs is a contributor to our preoccupation with sex. Sex is no guarantee of intimacy, anymore than a warm relationship leads necessarily to enjoyable sex. Thus, a common contributor to disappointing sex is expecting something from it which isn't there. You can never get enough of what you don't really want.

Many attempts at sex education and sex therapy would be more effective if we realized that many of the problems we address are not questions of "sexual" health, but problems of intimacy. Sex educators and therapists are increasingly recognizing that love therapy and love education may be even more useful then sex therapy and sex education as we attain greater understanding of the sources of "sexual" problems. Sexual health then, involves understanding the place of sexual desire and pleasure in the repertoire of human behaviors, overcoming those outmoded biases which impede sexual fulfillment, an assertive approach to meeting sexual needs, and a sensitivity to the rights of others. Sexual health is more than the successful working of our sexual plumbing or complying with irrelevant reproductivity based rules. It is the ability to express ourselves joyfully as unique sexual human beings touching ourselves and others in the fullest sense of the word.

# Addressing the Sexual Needs of Patients in Health Care Systems

David A. Shore, ACSW
Janice M. Pyrce, ACSW

Social work practice in health care is a diverse field encompassing various types of settings and service delivery systems. Within each setting, social workers may practice at different organizational levels including direct service, training, supervision, administration, consultation, planning, and research. The practice of social work therefore has great potential for impacting the increased responsiveness of a health care system to the sexual needs of patients. This article will examine the nature, organization and structure of social work in health care systems and the ways in which social workers can promote institutional change.

In order to discuss the impact social workers can have on systemic responsiveness to the sexual needs of patients, it is important to consider the conceptual base of social work which serves to position the profession in the challenging role of institutional agent. The mission of social work includes both a psycho-social approach to direct service and a belief in systems intervention. Activity on both of these levels can be effective in promoting a new organizational approach to patients, which includes an acknowledgement and belief in the patient's rights as a sexual being.

Social work, since its early days, has been practiced in health care settings. A historical review in this country begins with the invitation of a social worker, Ida M. Cannon, to Dr. Richard Cabot's clinic, at Massachusetts General Hospital, in 1903. Dr. Cabot was interested in the social worker acquiring information about the social conditions and personal problems of his patients. The social worker was also to act as a liaison between the hospital and other social service agencies. A social work program was later instituted at Johns Hopkins University in 1907. The conceptual base of social work was not well formulated in those days, with social workers

*21*

serving at the invitation of the host institution, under the direction of Medical Staff leadership.

As the knowledge base and skill repertoire of social workers grew and expanded through this century, so has the quality and pervasiveness of social work interventions within health care delivery systems. Despite its modest beginning in a hospital dispensary in Boston at the turn of the century, thousands of social workers in health settings have made significant, if not infrequently recognized contributions to the health and mental health of individuals, families and communities over the years. The National Association of Social Workers (N.A.S.W.) statistics document one third of its members practicing in health care or mental health settings (N.A.S.W., 1975). Schulman (1977) predicts the health/mental health field will become the employer of over 50% of all social workers in the next two decades. Between 1960 and 1970 alone the number of social workers employed in health care nearly doubled (Bracht, 1974). Of this contingency of health care social workers, approximately 70 percent hold a master's or higher degree (Bracht, 1978).

The health care systems in which this army of social workers practice include general medical-surgical hospitals, psychiatric hospitals, rehabilitation institutions, residential treatment facilities, long-term care facilities, out-patient clinics, community mental health centers, and family planning centers. Social workers practice in a multiplicity of positions within these health care systems. Differentially, each of these positions have great responsibility for expanding the orientation of health delivery systems to include attention to the sex-related needs of patients. By no means are all health care social workers direct line staff. Finney (1976) found, in a study of the academic backgrounds of professional staff in health planning agencies, that among staff-level planners social work represented the largest employed group and ranked third among directors and deputy directors of those planning agencies (Finney, Pessin, Matheis, 1976). This chapter will look at several of these positions and the specific ways in which institutional change can be affected by social workers.

## ROLE CONFUSION

Although there has been a lengthy history of social work participation in health care systems, issues, concerns and confusion abound on the specific roles and functions of social work in health care. Several studies (Blackey, 1956; Wolock and Russell, 1972; and Carrigan, 1978) have pointed out discrepancies between the self-perception by social workers of their roles as compared with the perception of the social work role as seen by other disciplines and by hospital administrators. The definitional problem of role and function faced by social workers in health care systems is in some ways inherent in the profession, and manifests in a variety of social work practice settings. The somewhat popular critique of social work "attempting to be all things to all people" contributes to the identity problem faced by social workers in all settings, but particularly in multi-disciplinary health care settings (Lister, 1980). There are numerous factors that contribute to the "hand-maiden dilemma" of health care social workers, and certainly there is much validity to the concern about professional identity and autonomy. The authors agree with Hallowitz (1972) that social workers share partial responsibility for their unsatisfactory role definitions. It is certain that multi-disciplinary settings breed certain professional frustrations. This article will attempt to illustrate areas, methods, and approaches for change.

## THE SOCIAL WORKER AS CHANGE AGENT

In regard to sex-related issues, social workers have a rightful place as that change agent. A profile of social work deployment in the health field shows that in most settings we are either a significant discipline in terms of our numerical representation, or indeed the largest provider group. In the mental health field for example, social work is by far the largest of the traditional professions providing services. A study by the National Institute of Mental Health (1972) uncovered that 42 percent of all staff of all mental health facilities are social workers (in contrast to psychiatrists, 30.7 percent; psychologists, 22.4 percent; and psychiatric nurses, 4.9 percent). In federally funded community mental health centers social work has an even larger percentage of the staffing pie, accounting for 44.8 percent of the professional provider work force (N.I.M.H., 1972).

Our deployment in the health care field having been established, we can close the circle for providing justification for the role of social workers in addressing sex-related issues in health settings by citing two non-social worker sex-researchers—Alfred Kinsey and William Masters. Kinsey indicated that social workers were involved in dealing with their clients' sexual problems even more often then were physicians (Kinsey, Martin, & Pomeroy, 1948). This finding was in keeping with that of William Masters (1970) who determined that 75 percent of all sexual problems for which help was sought in this country were treated by members of four professions other than medicine and that social work was one of these professions.

The above two practice realities come together in the most forceful statement of Harold Lief, Director of the Center for the Study of Sex Education in Medicine at the University of Pennsylvania. Dr. Lief notes "that the health practitioner should acquire basic skills in sex counseling is no longer in dispute" (Lief, 1979). While Dr. Lief contends that the role of the health practitioner in issues of human sexuality is no longer in dispute, nothing could be further from the truth. Responding to a patient's rights bill that was about to be introduced in the California legislature, a statute that would create a legal right to have sexual activity in acute care settings, the Editor of the prestigious journal, *Nursing Management* (1983) responded:

> In all honesty, I must say that this entire scenario is more than daunting, it's ridiculous. I am all for patient's rights, but enough is enough. Not only is enough enough, it is a surfeit. More than a surfeit, it is too much . . . That a hospital should provide opportunity for family—and even "great and good friends"—to reassure, comfort and express affection toward their loved ones, I can see, endorse and urge. That an acute care institution is required to provide a setting for "love in the afternoon" (evening, night or morning), I find a prodigious distortion of purpose and function. (Curtin, 1983)

A liberal interpretation of the statute would require acute care settings to accommodate all patients' desires to engage in the sexual activities of their choice without respect to marital status or sexual preference. Nurse Curtin believes that "private activities belong in private homes, apartments, motels, even bordellos, but not in public institutions. When a person must reside permanently, or for a long period of time, in an institution, adjustments should be made for private living in public places. However, there is a time and place for everything—"and an acute care hospital certainly is not the place even when patients have the time" (Curtin, 1983).

Nurse Curtin concludes by paraphrasing Samuel Pepys and suggesting that we put this statute "to bed." Throughout this text research and practice experiences suggesting the often critical role of human sexuality in the health care of patients is presented and therefore will not be duplicated at this time. The role of the institution and its effects on sex-related issues is also well documented and explored elsewhere (Shore, 1981a; 1981b; 1982).

Returning one final time to the Curtin editorial, we see that our editor has not missed the mark by very much. She suggests, albeit with a nervous humor, that if issues of human sexuality are to be addressed within the hospital setting, it does not remain the province of any one discipline or service. For example, under Infection Control the question is raised, "Will sexually transmitted diseases have to be added to the list of nosocomial infections? Could the institution be held liable for, perhaps a hospital-acquired case of herpes? If so, our duty is clear, and infection control committees must expand their surveillance in many new and interesting directions." With regard to Risk Management this question is put forth, "And what about possible pregnancies? eviscerations? cracked vertebrae? surely Risk Management will entangle itself in the intricacies of these issues." Materials Management raises the following one liners, "When I try to contemplate the eventual involvement of the physical therapy department, my sensory neurons overload. Shall the whirlpool become the hot tub? The exercise mats play pens? And the potential applications of massage therapy and so on go far beyond the resources of my limited fantasy life."

Finally, with regard to Quality Assurance, the editor proposes a rating scale, asking patients to rate the sexual services received according to the following scale:

- libidinous
- lucious
- lackluster
- lackadaisical
- lustless
- listless
- lifeless
- ludicrous

Ironically the authors recall the use of similar humor masking anxiety when schools of social work were beginning to offer courses in human sexuality. Colleagues would ask the instructor if there was field work, homework, extra credit assignments, etc. As our comfort level with sexuality increased, the number of sex jokes deceased, to the point that issues of human sexuality are now accepted and occasionally well integrated within the social work curriculum. Similarly when one writes an editorial about sex in health care settings a decade from now, one would expect far less anxious humor. The fact is that no one is suggesting that patients be permitted to "come and go" as they wish sexually any more than patients independently write their own treatment plans. Rather, as is pointed out throughout this volume, sex-related issues can play an integral part in the education and clinical care of patients. The authors are not suggesting that sex magically enter health settings via a sexologist per se (or as the editorial suggests, via contracting with an experienced consultant such as the madame from Texas' famous Chicken Ranch). Rather, the authors are suggesting a format not dissimilar to that suggested by Nurse Curtin, institutionalizing sex-related aspects of hospitalization via already existing mechanisms. The remainder of this article will seek to identify some of the ways in which social workers at various levels of intervention can identify the sexual needs of patients as well as respond to these needs.

## IDENTIFYING NEED

Health care systems are complicated organizations. It is a challenge for the organization to remain sensitive to the psycho-social needs of the individual served. From the beginning of this century social workers in health care have been concerned about responding to patients in a holistic fashion. A first step in considering institutional change is to compile a needs assessment of the patient population served. An inventory of the sex-related needs of the patient population, and the current approach to needs satisfaction can be a beginning point of analysis. Such an assessment can be conducted by social workers at all levels of practice within the health care system. It can be conducted through utilizing already existing intake instruments, surveys, review procedure, and research.

### Intake

At intake, initial data is gathered about the individual seeking services. The specific data gathered varies by setting but generally includes a description of the presenting problem, information on history and the precipitant of the problem, and data on previous attempts at resolution. Intake provides an excellent opportunity to explore a client's sexual needs. This data can provide further understanding of the presenting problem and can contribute to more effective treatment planning.

Settings often have an intake guide sheet. A simple change approach is to propose the inclusion of a section on sexual needs in the interview format. This can often be accomplished through a written memo proposing an expansion in intake data collection. The psychosocial approach, well documented in social work literature, can be utilized to support the data collection expansion. In many settings the intake guide sheet is developed and designed by the Director of Social Service who maintains decision-making authority on inclusion categories.

The second step of this change process is the implementation of the expanded interview format. It is well to point out that an important variable in conducting successful intake interviews is the skill of the interviewer. One component impacting effectiveness is the comfort level of a worker with the area being covered, and the specific information gathered. The authors believe it is important to develop an implementation plan which will assist workers in understanding their own feelings and reactions in gathering information on sexual needs, issues and concerns. It is certain that a worker's own discomfort level will be conveyed to the client. This situation will make it quite difficult to gather data (Hallowitz and Shore, 1978).

## ORGANIZATIONAL CHANGE

Social workers at all levels of an organization can impact organizational change. Social workers in administrative and consulting roles can assist in the determination of specific hospital programs and specific policies and procedures that serve to meet the sexual needs of the patient. As has been noted above, health care organizations are complex systems. An understanding of both systems theory and organization theory can be helpful for the social worker in an administrative or a consulting position who wishes to impact institutional change. One approach to planning change is to review existing mechanisms or avenues which can be utilized in promoting change. The authors believe there are potential vehicles for promoting change within organizations.

## Vehicles for Change

### Committees

Hospital wide committees are one area for social workers to participate in order to promote organizational changes. Often hospitals will have a planning committee or a policy and procedure committee that may serve as a vehicle for having certain policies and procedures or programs introduced.

### Quality Assurance

Since its introduction by the Joint Commission on Accreditation of Hospitals (J.C.A.H.) in 1979, quality assurance programming is an integral, coordinated effort to problem solve, which utilizes broad-based staff participation. Components of the quality assurance program include staff growth and development, utilization review, patient care monitoring, and program evaluation. Each of these components can be an area in which an institution's lack of attention to a patient's sexual needs can be identified, assessed, and a change proposed, implemented and monitored. The beauty of a well-organized quality assurance program is that it provides a structure for staff input into problem-solving. In essence it confronts the powerlessness feeling of an individual in a large system.

### Educational Programs

The literature on human sexuality has well documented the need for sex education. A clinician in the initial meeting with a couple experiencing sexual dysfunction difficulties may find that the major problem is a lack of knowledge about sexual anatomy and physiology. Reflecting on growing up, it is easy to remember how sex can be the "elephant in the closet." Everyone is aware it is around, yet no one dares to talk directly about it. Relative to sexuality in health care settings, the educational process is twofold. Attention to both staff and patient education programs can have tremendous impact on enhancing an organization's approach to human sexuality.

Staff education. Continuing staff education is an integral part of many health care systems and is required by the Joint Commission on Accreditation of Hospitals. The staff growth and development standards of the J.C.A.H. require both orientation and staff development programs. The staff development programs must reflect all administrative and services changes in the facility. Also notable is the requirement that results of patient care evaluations or quality assurance activities be an important part of staff development programs. As has been noted previously, quality assurance can be an excellent vehicle for change, and particularly when the results of a patient care monitoring staffing, for example, becomes the basis for a staff education program addressing the sexual needs of patients.

Effective health care staff education on human sexuality should include three elements: 1) knowledge base, 2) affective component, and 3) specific assessment and treatment skills (Hallowitz and Shore, 1978). Social work practitioners in health care settings require a broad-based knowledge of human sexuality. It is also important that practitioners achieve a level of personal comfort with the content area—which generally requires some amount of introspection into one's own beliefs, experiences, and reactions. Small group interaction can be useful in providing an educational situation conducive to discussion, and an atmosphere in which attention can be given to affective concerns. The third element described above, specific assessment and treatment skills, also requires staff development training. Increasingly, schools of social work are incorporating human sexuality into curriculums although the authors believe it is safe to say that the average practitioner leaving social work school may be in need of additional training relative to interviewing, assessing, developing treatment plans, and implementing treatment plans as they relate to sexual issues.

*Patient education.* Increasing numbers of organizations are developing "wellness programs" for employees, clients, and patients. Wellness programs are generally thought of as preventive or enrichment programs on a specific topic. The nature and goals of wellness programs are such that inclusion of education on human sexuality should be consistent with these goals and objectives. Wellness programs have gained increased momentum in recent years in business and health care circles and may prove to be an excellent area for social workers to integrate human sexuality.

## SUMMARY

It is a well accepted tenet of training in both the field of social work and human sexuality that the successful practitioner must master the cognitive, affective, and skill components that interface with his or her work. The authors have attempted to highlight some of the organizational variables that are particuliarly idiosyncratic to health care and therefore require special attention. While health care has frequently been accused of "system rigidity," and while social workers must negotiate a multi-disciplinary hierarchy, organized health care, almost uniquely (for social workers), has institutionalized change agents including those identified throughout this article.

Given our historical and contemporary concern with the *total person,* it is hoped that social workers will take the lead in introducing, as appropriate, sexual issues in the care of their patients and clients. Such a change is perhaps never more appropriate than when those in our care reside in our *total institutions.*

## REFERENCES

Blackey, E. Social work in the hospital: A sociological approach. *Social Work,* 1956, 1(3), 43-48.
Bracht, N. Health care: The largest human service system. *Social Work,* 1974, 19(5), 532-542.
Bracht, N. The scope and historical development of social work, 1900-1975. In N. Bracht, (Ed.) *Social work in health care: A guide to professional practice.* New York: The Haworth Press, 1978, p. 3.
Carrigan, Z. Social workers in medical settings: Who defines us? *Social Work,* 1972, 17, 89-97.
Curtin, L.L. Sex in the hospital. *Nursing Management,* 1983, 14(6), 9-10.
Finney, R., Pessin, R. & Matheis, L. Prospects for social workers in health planning. *Health and Social Work.* 1976, 1(3), 7-26.
Hallowitz, E. Innovation in hospital social work. *Social Work,* 1972, 17, 89-97.
Hallowitz, E. & Shore, D.A. Small-group process in teaching human sexuality. *Health and Social Work,* 1978, 3(4), 132-151.
Joint Commission on Accreditation of Hospitals. *Consolidated standards manual for child, adolescent, and adult psychiatric, alcoholism, and drug abuse facilities.* Chicago: J.C.A.H., 1981, 45-46.
Kinsey, A., Martin, C., & Pomeroy, W. *Sexual Behavior in the Human Male.* Philadelphia: W.B. Saunders, 1948.
Lief, H. Why sex education for health practitioners? In Green, R. (Ed.) *Human Sexuality A health practitioners text.* Baltimore: The Williams & Wilkins Company, 1979, p. 3.
Lister, L. Role expectations of social workers and other health professionals. *Health and Social Work,* 1980, 5(2), 41-49.
Masters, W. Repairing the conjugal bed. *Time,* May 25, 1970.
National Association of Social Workers. *Manpower Data Bank Frequency Distribution.* Washington: Mimeographed, 1975, p. 4.
National Institute of Mental Health. *Staffing of Mental Health Facilities,* Washington D.C., 1972, table 1.6, pg. 35.
Shore, D.A. *Sex-related issues in correctional facilities.* Chicago: The Playboy Foundation, 1981(b).
Shore, D.A. Sexual abuse and sexual education in child-caring institutions. *Journal of Social Work & Human Sexuality,* 1982, 1(1/2) 177-184.
Shore, D.A., & Gochros, H.L. *Sexual problems of adolescents in institutions.* Springfield, Illinois: Charles C. Thomas, 1981(a).

Shulman, L. Social work education for health practice, *Social Work in Health Care,* 1979, 2(4).

United States Department of Health, Education and Welfare. *Health Resources Document,* Washington D.C., 1971.

Wolock, I. & Russell, Harry. Physician's views and use of social services. *The Journal of Perth Amboy General Hospital,* 1972, 32-40.

# System Linkage:
# Dealing with Sexual Issues
# in a Case Management Approach

Larry Lister, DSW

Among the traditional functions of social workers are those activities which help to link clients with various resources. Social work actually evolved out of the urban experience, where dislocations of people resulted from the gradual differentiation of life systems into separate entities such as the nuclear family, the school, the job, the health care system and all of the other divisions of modern life. Social work intervention is directed toward each of these systems in two ways: first, it is focused on the internal processes of each system and, second, it functions to help connect these often diverse systems. Thus it is that a social worker in a health setting must not only be able to carry out tasks within that setting, but also to know what is offered in the way of services in the internal structures of the other health and welfare systems and to be able to help link the client with those services.

In order to accomplish these linkage functions, a number of separate roles and strategies are available to the social worker. As shown in the introductory chapter, those direct practice roles which consist of brokerage, mediation, negotiation and advocacy are all relevant to helping connect clients with resource systems. While all of these roles may be carried out separately, they each are relevant to the increasingly important role of case manager or case coordinator. Consequently, this chapter will focus on a description of some of the system-linkage roles as these may be performed by the social worker when implementing the case management process.

*33*

## CASE MANAGEMENT*

Increasingly there is a literature about case management and some beginning evaluation of the results of this approach (Bertsche and Horejsi, 1980; Johnson and Rubin, 1983; Benjamin, n.d.). Case management has special relevance for those clients for whom long-term planning and coordination is necessary to help sustain social functioning at the highest level. Some of the situations where case management is most relevant are: child welfare (where parents are not able to provide care and planning), the aging (especially where members of the family are unavailable or unable to assume responsibility), for the chronically disabled (either the physically disabled or the mentally or intellectually impaired), and for those clients where long-term intervention is required due to the nature of a health problem (i.e., stroke or terminal illness).

## THE BRACES MODEL

In developing a model of case management, this author created the acronym BRACES as a way to identify the essential components in the case management process. This model will be discussed and some illustrations will be used to show how the model is applicable for dealing with sex-related issues.

The dictionary identifies the word *brace* as "something that connects" and "to make stronger" and "something that transmits, directs, resists, or supports weight or pressure" and "a mark used to connect words or items to be considered together" (Webster's, Note 1). The connotation of these various definitions is what is meant by the BRACES acronym, since it is meant to suggest a process which helps to support, to bring together, and to undergird.

The basic case management model is one where the social worker is designated as the person who will be in charge of the BRACES process with respect to a designated client. As case manager, the social worker is the ultimately responsible professional who is accountable for seeing that a planned process of assistance is carried out by the various parties who are relevant to the case situation. The components of the BRACES model are: *B*ehavioral Specificity,

---

*Case management tends to be an unfortunate title, since it implies a control of clients. As actually illustrated in the literature, however—and as presented in the model to be discussed in this chapter—it is a model which depends on cooperative efforts.

Resources, Accountability, Coordination, Evaluation and System. In application, then, the BRACES model is as follows:

## Behavioral Specificity

In implementing case management, the behaviors to be performed by at least three contributors to the process are made as specific as possible. The three contributors are: (1) the client/family members, (2) the case manager and (3) other service providers. The behavior of each of these is negotiated, clarified and made known to each other party involved in the specific management situation. Thus, a father who was removed from the home because of incest must be made aware of the on-going, process behaviors and the final, outcome behaviors which will demonstrate his ability to assure his child protection from further sexual abuse (Conte & Berliner, 1981). Not only do the father and all other family members need to understand their behavior, but the other two components of the service-client system also have to be clear about their service activities. Thus, it must be clear to all that the case manager will coordinate the process, while the other service provider(s) will each perform their contracted portion of the total service plan. If the parents are to attend weekly therapy sessions, then their therapist's approach to individual and/or couple therapy is made a part of the service plan. The purpose for specifying the behaviors for all three sub-systems is to assure that both self and other expectations are clear and to also build-in the concept of case management as a process of mutual effort.

## Resources

Case management depends on the availability of resources from two existing sources: (1) the agency/system within which the case manager is located, and (2) the community. A third source must be considered as well—this being whatever systems there are which can be used to produce a new and needed resource. To briefly elaborate the resources component, the case manager is usually located within a service system; i.e., a hospital, long-term care facility, department of public social services. Most of these systems have their own resources which are available to meet the needs of clients and the case manager connects the clients with these intra-system services. Many resources are not within the internal network of the case manager's own service system; thus, other of the linkage activities discussed in this chapter are necessary to connect the client system outward to the relevant community systems which are available.

Not uncommonly, the community does not have the resources which are necessary to meet the needs of large numbers of clients. The direct practice social worker is in a unique position—based on accumulated information from many cases—of identifying problems which call for action at the policy level. A recent case in point is the rapidly accumulating evidence of the devastating impact of AIDS (Acquired Immune Deficiency Syndrome) on gay men in various parts of the country (Acevedo, Note 2). As the evidence has accumulated both on local and national levels, social workers have been alerting each other about the growing evidence of the syndrome, and have urged contact with national legislators in order to make increased money available for epidemiological research on the problem. At this writing, there is no evidence of what has been the unique contribution by social workers to this political effort (since many other groups have advocated for funds), but increased attention has been devoted to the problem as pressure has been exerted from various sources around the country. While, as this example shows, there are times when resources do not exist for the problem at hand, the case management approach helps to highlight the need for social workers at all service levels to provide the documentation needed for resource development.

When resources are available, however, it is the essence of the case management process to help make the connections between these sources of supplies—which are material as well as emotional—and the clients who need them. Since the case manager does not always offer clinical intervention to clients—and since the case manager must often use other outside community resources—the skills, techniques and processes involved in case management are those which help to create the client linkage with resources. In order to accomplish this linkage, the roles of broker, advocate, mediator and negotiator are available to the case manager. These roles will be described below, with examples of how these are useful for meeting the sex-related needs of patients.

## Broker

The activity of the social worker as broker differs from the tasks which a worker performs when making a referral, yet the distinction seems not always clear. In referral, the social worker is moving the client into a new service system. This is, of course, a linkage function, since it creates a contact between the client and a resource. However, once the referral process is complete, the referring social worker is no longer involved in the case.

Brokerage, on the other hand, is a most relevant activity to the case management process because in this role the social worker is maintaining contact with the client system and is also creating one or a series of connections between the client and other resources. The brokering activity stems from the worker's assessment and coordinated planning with the client(s). As such, the social worker maintains the overriding focus on how resources are helping to stabilize and strengthen the clients' capacities and are helping to achieve the goals which have been agreed upon in the case. The brokering model is akin to what a stockbroker does for his/her clients; he/she anticipates, assesses, makes suggestions and buys and sells on behalf of his/her clients, all with the aim of helping them maximize the financial component of their lives. In a similar way, the social work broker acts to help maximize client's lives by anticipating needs, keeping alert to possible resources which will help move the client toward planned goals, and by helping create the linkage between client and resources which will enrich—not the financial—but the psychosocial aspects of the client's life.

To illustrate how the brokerage function may enhance the sexuality of a client, consider the issues of identity and sex activity—two of the "spheres" identified as part of the definition of sexuality in the introductory chapter—as these have relevance for a middle-aged man who is diagnosed as having diabetes:

> In preparation for social work with a diabetic, the case manager would need to know about the sexual implications of diabetes mellitus. The literature reports more than a 50% increase in the incidence of diabetes mellitus in the U.S. in the past 10 years, partly due to improved treatment and longer life span (Schiavi, 1979). The prevalence of impotence varies with age; 29% of men below age 30 who are diabetic have been shown to experience erectile disorder, while 40% to 73% of men with the disease in their 60s were found to be impotent in various studies (Schiavi, 1979). Careful evaluation must be done by members of the health care team with each patient, since impotence may appear in the first year following diagnosis and disappear subsequently. For example, Woods (1975) cites data showing 70% of males impotent in the year following

diagnosis, while 45% are impotent after a diabetes duration of over five years. Thus, medical evaluation must help determine physiologic bases for impotence, while psychosocial evaluation must help determine emotional origins or complications. When there is a diagnosis of irreversible impotence, there are various options available to the patient. Individual assessment and intervention must focus on which approaches will be most acceptable, feasible and practicable for a given patient. In addition, extensive couples' therapy between the male and his partner—and intersystemic brokering—may be required, as illustrated in the following case:

Mr. T., a man in his early 60s, had suffered from impotence for some months before being diagnosed as diabetic. Unfortunately, during that time he had tried to cope with his faltering sexual ability by repeated attempts at intercourse with his wife, a woman who was at least 15 years younger than he. The more he attempted without results, the more both he and his wife became distressed. By the time Mr. T. had acceded to his wife's requests to seek medical attention, the marriage had begun to deteriorate, with Mrs. T. wishing to avoid her husband and Mr. T. becoming increasingly suspicious that his wife was becoming interested in a colleague at her work. When the social worker was finally called into the case, a great deal of effort was needed to improve the T's communication processes. When exploring the T's current sexual adjustment, it became clear that in Mr. T's value system, a man was not "a man" unless he could satisfy his wife sexually, and sexual satisfaction was only achieved through intercourse.

The social worker explored the attitudes of both Mr. and Mrs. T. in separate appointments and learned that Mrs. T. generally felt that sex was her husband's pleasure and that a limited sex life was fulfilling to her as long as Mr. T. was not in the emotional agony of recent months. The social worker ascertained that Mrs. T. had no sexual interest in any of her colleagues at work; her main problem was her husband's insistence on sexual performance and his depression and self-loathing when he was not able to achieve an erection.

In the separate interview with Mr. T. it was clear that intercourse was the measure of sexuality for him. Explorations by the social worker of alternative means of satisfaction (i.e., oral-genital, manual stimulation) were rejected out of hand by

Mr. T.; in fact, the social worker needed to carefully explain the reasons for the questions and discussion with Mr. T, since Mr. T. began to express negative reactions about the social worker for even discussing sexuality in such terms. The social worker then carried out the brokerage aspects of the case management process by arranging for Mr. T. to discuss feasible remedial measures with several other members of the health care system. Among the choices presented to him, Mr. T. learned of two types of penile implants which are currently available. The first type, sponge-filled silicone rods, are surgically implanted and are not painful but have the disadvantage of remaining permanently semi-erect. The second type, also surgically implanted, are inflatable by a process of tubes carrying a solution from a hollow cylinder which is sutured to the abdominal wall (Wood and Rose, 1978). As reported by Schiavi: "in our experience, implantation of penile prostheses in selected patients with organic impotence can result in significant improvement of the psychological and sexual status of the individual" (Schiavi, Note 3). The author continues: "Factors that should be taken into consideration when considering implantation of a prosthesis are the organic basis of the sexual disorder, a satisfactory marital relationship, a pre-diabetic history of adequate sexual adjustment, the maintenance of sexual drive, and unimpaired orgastic capacity" (Schiavi, Note 4). In the T. case, the above criteria seemed to all be met, with the possible exception of the marital relationship; however, the evaluation indicated that the marriage had been fully satisfactory to both partners prior to the concern with the impotence.

As a result of the discussion with the physician, Mr. T. was unequivocably in favor of the first type of implant described. This device seemed least complicated to him and given his age and the nature of his total life activity, the permanent semi-erection was felt to be no barrier to him. At the time of this case, in the community in which the Ts lived, there was no surgeon who was performing this type of surgery. Consequently, the social worker further acted as broker by working with the physician to find out where the surgery could be performed. Because Mr. T. had begun to develop a good relationship with the social worker (facilitated by the worker's careful approach to the discussion of the sexual issues, which were the first such discussions by Mr. T. in his life!), the social worker made contact with the social worker at the hospital where the surgery was to be performed and, with Mr. T's full knowledge and concurrence, prepared the new worker for meeting and working with both Mr. and Mrs. T. upon their arrival. As noted, Mrs. T. was brought fully into the entire process, partly in order to enhance the marital re-adjustment but to also encourage her activities as "broker" in the natural network.

It is of relevance in this example to note that the physician in the initial setting was not an advocate of penile implantation. In fact, that physician was not predisposed to deal with the sexual issue at all, other than to go along with Mr. T's own denial and inability to discuss his concerns and to assume that the Ts would probably abstain from sexual activity, the latter assumption based on the belief that Mr. T. was in his early 60s and was probably losing interest anyway! It was therefore not only necessary for the social worker to carefully maneuver discussion with the patient in an area which was causing inordinate stress but to also cautiously approach the subject with the patient's physician. When Mr. T.—based on full consideration of all alternatives—made *his* decision about how he preferred to handle his impotence, the social worker acted as broker by facilitating the process whereby the patient received the medical attention of his choice. Since long-term medical care was required for both the diabetes and other health problems of Mr. T., case management was a relevant approach, with brokerage a necessary component.

## Advocate

Much has been written about the advocate role of the social worker (Sosin and Caulum, 1983), a role which can have relevance for meeting the sexual needs of clients. Advocacy may be of three types; (1) *case,* where activity is carried out on behalf of a specific client, (2) *class,* in which the social worker agitates for a defined group (i.e., the need for sex education for disabled children) and (3) *cause,* where an issue not necessarily focused on a specific client or a defined group is the focus (for example, the need for legislation to continue to provide funding for family planning services available to any consumer).

In a discussion of case advocacy on behalf of children, McGowan notes how the advocacy function may be relatively simple in instances where the advocate knows there will ultimately be success because the situation involves a clear denial of client rights, as contrasted with the situation where the advocate's success "depends on the good will of respondents in the target system" (McGowan, note 5). In order to appreciate the complexity of the advocacy process—and illustrating the ways in which different social work roles overlap—McGowan lists six methods of advocacy intervention and some of the means by which the methods are implemented. The six methods are: (1) intercession (request, plead, persist); (2) persuasion (inform, instruct, clarify, explain, argue); (3) negotiation (dialogue, bargain, placate); (4) pressure (threaten, challenge, disregard); (5) coercion (deceive, disrupt, administrative redress, legal action); and (6) indirect (client education or training, community organizing, third-party intervention, system dodging, constructing alternatives) (McGowan, 1978). As can be seen by this list, advocacy can consist of some rather benign influencing strategies or can be represented by considerable force and disruption.

As anyone has learned in attempting to use advocacy approaches, the contexts in which advocacy is applied must be carefully considered in order to assure maximum gain not only on the single occasion, but in anticipation of the next occasions when the social worker will need to use the advocate role in order to accomplish system linkage. For example, the use of disruptive tactics not only unsettles systems for the period of their use, but leaves traces of resistance which will act as impediments to future efforts of that social worker, no matter how much less aggressive the subsequent methods. This is not to suggest a preference for one strategy over another, but the literature is simply not sufficient in reports of outcomes of advocacy approaches to provide definitive guidelines. There is, in fact, sometimes the implication that all that social workers need to do is to agitate for the needs of their clients and systems will yield. Then, when social workers find that systems are much stronger than even the might of the rightest worker, they may be too burned (not necessarily burned-out) to attempt advocacy approaches in the future when such approaches are again needed.

Several strategies on behalf of patients in long-term care settings may be cited as examples of advocacy on behalf of the sexuality of both younger and elderly persons.

A first example concerns the situation of an elderly married couple who both entered a long-term care setting around the same time. Under the impetus of the patient's Bill of Rights, consideration was given to not only their preferences for how they would be housed in the facility, but as well to their continuing needs for intimacy. It was determined by several staff members from various disciplines that there was a strong desire on the part of the couple to continue to sleep together; however, for various health and practical reasons it was not possible for the couple to share a bed. The concerned staff, acting as advocates for the couple, were able to convince others that a bed could be fashioned of mattresses which could be placed on the floor (issues of cleanliness and other objections having been taken care of) and the couple helped to be able to sleep together on any of the nights in which either of them indicated an interest. To be sure, there was some initial chuckling among staff about making the arrangements—and there was some questioning of the motives of the staff advocates—but before long, as it became clear how important it was for the elderly couple to sleep together (it was the comfort of their bodies near each other which had been the reason for their request), no staff member found the arrangement noteworthy.

The above is an example of case advocacy on behalf of the assessed needs of particular clients. The example to follow illustrates the use of class advocacy on behalf of a potential group of consumers.*

Also under the stimulus of the Patients' Bill of Rights a number of activities were initiated in order to create a private place for patients in a skilled nursing facility. At a training session when the Bill was first being promoted, a skilled nursing home administrator from another institution complained publicly about how he had allocated over $5,000 in his facility for a ''sex room'' and none of the patients ever used it! Staff—upon hearing the other administrator's discussion and

---

*The example actually reflects the system-development function of social workers, since it is not concerned with linkage of clients to existing resources, but is reported here because it illustrates the contrast with the case advocacy level and is a form of advocacy which is appropriate for the direct practice social worker.

some of the reactions of others attending the training—realized that to create any such resource in their own institution would require careful planning. In initial discussions with the patient care planning committee in their facility, the idea was broached of a "patients' room," the purpose of which would be for patients to have a place of privacy where they could go alone or with someone of their choosing and where there would not be a label attached to the room's purpose. Subsequent to an initial receptivity on the part of the committee, a small sub-group of staff began to formulate ideas for the development of the "patients' room." This sub-group was led by the social worker who had taken on the advocacy for the development of this new intra-system resource. Realizing that resistance could likely come from any part of the system, the sub-committee moved slowly into consideration of where in the facility the room could be located, what furnishings it would have, where the money would come from for the furnishings, how patients who needed assistance in mobility would be able to reach such a room, how staff would keep informed when a patient might be using the room without the patient feeling self-conscious or supervised, and similar practical questions. Early in the process, administration either expressed their own interest in the project or were co-opted through incurring their participation in some aspect of the project (i.e., helping to designate a location for the room). A significant hurdle was met when objections were raised by some of the nursing and housekeeping staff that they were "not going to be changing linens" after residents had used the room. This objection was dealt with as reasonable, and the committee developed a procedure whereby any patient using the room would be responsible for leaving it in the same condition as it was found. This meant that linens would be placed in a hamper and fresh linens put on the bed, ash trays would be cleaned, bottles would be placed in a container, etc. Again, since the resource was a "patient's room" there was not a focus on a single purpose for its use, but in drawing up a list of "rules" (in the manner that a motel posts its rules on the guest room doors), one of its purposes was specified as for intimacy and privacy when a patient wanted to be alone or close with another person. A humorous note to the planning process occurred when the rules were first tentatively discussed in the patient care committee; one of the highest administrative persons blurted out that "we are not going to run a house of prostitution around here" after the social worker pointed out that the language of the rules did not specify only "married couples" when designating the room as available for intimate contact.

As illustrated by the above example, the advocacy process utilized a number of the methods and strategies designated by McGowan such as persuasion, negotiation, construction of alternatives, and patient and staff education (McGowan, 1978). Especially since the advocacy effort was intra-organizational, great care needed to be taken with respect to which tactics were used, lest credibility be compromised for the future.

## Mediation and Negotiation

*Negotiation* is a process which involves gaining the greatest benefits for people through the use of (1) information, (2) time and (3) power (Cohen, 1980). In Cohen's discussion of the component of power in negotiation, he identifies a number of sources such as competition, risk-taking, knowledge of the others' needs, ability to reward and punish, persistence and expertise. In terms of a strategy for demonstrating expertise, Cohen points out the need to early establish one's background credentials and knowledge so that other parties will begin to respect- and defer to- that expertise. Because: (1) the component of a patient's sexuality is frequently overlooked,* and (2) health care providers can be reluctant to introduce sexual issues for reasons of their own discomfort, and (3) in-depth or comprehensive knowledge of sexuality is frequently lacking in any single provider, and (4) no single discipline on the health care team has traditionally been assigned all the sexual components in the assessment and treatment of patients—for these reasons, the social worker may garner leverage for negotiation by establishing expertise in the sexual area.

Unlike negotiation (at least in the model presented by Cohen)— where the social worker is attempting to achieve maximal gain for the client, or advocacy, there the worker is clearly established as a partisan in a no-compromise effort—in *mediation* the social worker

---

*For example, Wagner and Sivarajan (1979) describe a medical study where detailed data were elicited from coronary patients about swimming, dancing, climbing stairs—even sailing as crew—but with no mention of sexual activity.

assumes an objective position between two or more parties to help them arrive at the most individually and mutually agreeable resolution of an impasse or conflict. In this role, the social work activity is much more focused on eliciting information, on remaining objective, on helping all parties to understand and express their needs and preferences, and on the careful transmission of information between the parties or on the monitoring and guiding of the discussion in a face to face encounter. Some of the procedures used in the problem-solving phase of mediation include "joint meetings, shuttle diplomacy, caucus . . . negotiation techniques or creative problem solving methods" (Chandler, 1983). Frequently, mediation involves the management of strong components of hostility and dissention which are felt by one or more of the parties to the conflict. However, as presented here, the mediator role may simply best describe the social worker's stance which is most relevant when the goal is the greatest felt gain—and least felt loss—on the part of all parties. In this way the mediator role contrasts with the greater partisanship and manipulative strategies involved with the advocate and negotiator roles, though, as noted, in actual practice these roles frequently overlap or are performed in combination.

The following example illustrates how the social worker may use negotiation and mediation strategies on behalf of a patient and several of the patient's significant others, including members of the health care team.

In separate interviews with the patient—a man in his early 50s who had been hospitalized for a myocardial infarction—the social worker elicited the patient's great anxiety about resuming sexual activity. The patient's anxiety was reflective of several "spheres" of sexuality; (1) intimacy with his wife and his own ability to continue to experience sensual pleasure, (2) his identity and role as a male and (3) his lack of information about the physiological impact when he resumed sexual activity. The social worker matter-of-factly indicated that the patient's concerns were an expected component of care planning and would be brought up for discussion with the team when planning for the patient's long-term care.

With the patient's concurrence, the social worker "negotiated" the patient's needs with the health care team. Fully cognizant of the physician's expertise in the physiological area, the social worker nonetheless introduced the subject of the patient's need for information about the physical implications of the heart disease. The social worker demonstrated his own knowledge (and thus his "power" for negotiation) in this area with information such as that provided by Masters and Johnson that respiratory rate during intercourse increases only briefly (Masters and Johnson, 1966) and data about male physiological responses to different positions during sexual intercourse, including the suggestion that the popular myth of heart attacks during intercourse may be attributable to those men who are trying to "prove" themselves, as illustrated by a Japanese study where 25% of sudden deaths during coitus occurred in hotel rooms among men who were involved in extramarital relations with women who were much younger than themselves (Woods, 1975).

The mediator component in this case is illustrated by the social worker's intervention with the patient and his wife. Not only heart patients, but their sexual partners, are often anxious about the resumption of sexual activity. In the case under discussion, a component of mediation took place when the social worker helped process information between the patient, his wife and various health-team members. The wife needed to express some of her own anxiety and concern in private sessions with the social worker, since she was fearful that her anxieties might cause her husband to feel "put down" or as though she was treating him like an "old man." It was in the selective transmission of information between the various parties involved—helping the couple to gradually express their fears and helping various members of the health team to intervene in the areas of their expertise—that aspects of negotiation and mediation were carried out.

### Accountability

Case management demands accountability from all three of the groups who are participants in the process: the client/family, the case manager and each of the other service providers involved in a given case. Contracts, agreements, service plans and other recording devices are available or can be constructed for the purpose of helping to make clear, in writing, the goals and means for activities in a case (Maluccio and Marlow, 1974). Accountability, then, is the implementation of agreed upon plans and is not to be confused with the same thing as effectiveness, much as all efforts are directed toward effective solutions. The criterion for accountability is simply that each party involved in the case management process is held accountable for any tasks which they agree to carry out. Consequently, if a physician has been designated as the person to provide contraceptives to a willing mentally retarded woman, (all persons who are to be held accountable sign the service plan as a way of documenting their involvement), then the physician becomes the person all providers hold accountable. If the client's appropriate use of the contraceptive is to be monitored by the case manager, then the case manager is held accountable.

By the examples cited, it can be seen that case management is a highly visible process. Each participant is aware of what each other is doing and in this way accountability is furthered, since the participant who fails to carry out the tasks which he/she has contracted to carry becomes visible to a group of participants, with all of the possible means of sanction which that visibility may call forth.

## *Coordination*

Case management is the process of coordination of resources which help to meet a client's need or solve a client's problem(s). Indeed, much of the impetus for a case management approach stems from the desire to avoid the problems which too frequently occur when various service systems work at cross-purposes, as happens when there is no clearly designated central authority. In order to make the coordination workable and visible, it may be necessary to have one or more face to face meetings of clients and service providers to both plan the process of service delivery and to monitor progress in the implementation of agreed upon plans. Such meetings should, wherever possible, include the client(s), since the ultimate outcome most concerns them and since their active participation is so necessary to case progress.

One objection to having clients join in a case planning conference is that there may be dissension among various service providers about the direction to take in the case situation and that such disagreement should not be observed by the client. In practice, team functioning may be enhanced by training (Takamura et al., 1979). Additionally, there needs to be careful thought as to whether the objection is really because of its impact on clients or rather reflects differences in values, power, and approaches of the various parties in the case management process. This process may actually pull together some rather strange "bedfellows," and combinations of service providers who are not the usual mental health professionals may be the most relevant persons to involve in planning, as shown in the following example:

> Mrs. C. was a middle-aged divorced woman who had endured multiple assaults to her physical self, including several cancer surgeries (one requiring a mastectomy) followed by paralysis of the lower part of her body. Emotionally, she was a model for other patients and an inspiration to the health care team. In planning for her return home following discharge from the hospital, all of the appropriate follow-up home care health resources were mobilized. It was Mrs. C. who introduced the idea of creating some system whereby she could get herself in and out of her own bed, since she could not depend on her manfriend to lift her, since he too was disabled. Therefore, the care planning team was expanded to include an engineer and home remodeler who were able to create a system of hoists and pulleys which Mrs. C. could use to transfer from her wheelchair to her bed and thereby simultaneously both enhance her autonomy, while also providing means of maintaining her capacity for intimacy.

## Evaluation

Evaluation is another component of the case management approach. Evaluation is built in by the previously discussed requirements for behavioral specificity, clear goals and an accountability structure. All aspects of the case management process are structured in such a way as to make evaluation an integral component. The initial plans, or in-puts, are evaluated by each party of the contract. The thru-put portion—the activities used to move toward the terminal case goals—are monitored by the case manager. The reaching of final goals, and the setting of time tables for their achievement, become a form of outcome evaluation. As noted earlier, the position of the case manager makes it possible to evaluate from both single and accumulated cases, so that their progress and outcome become a source of information for the push for new community resources or for different therapeutic approaches, when it has become clear that a certain approach has not borne results in numbers of cases.

An example of the use of evaluation is the one reported by Hardgrove, documenting how a networking of services was created by a YWCA as an outcome of attempts to provide comprehensive help for a girl who was raped. (Hardgrove, 1976). The victim, a client in a delinquency diversion project, needed extensive advocacy in order to secure services for her, since few rape victims were appearing for help at that point in time in the community being described, and services were largely non-existent. In a good example of both the system maintenance and linkage roles, the experience with this one case led to the development of extensive coordination efforts and to new referral patterns, staff training for personnel in various hospitals and other community agencies (including the police), medical protocols for use in rape evaluation and treatment, a hotline of volunteers (some bilingual), and the development of a mutual support group, and advocacy activities, among the volunteers.

## System

System is the final component of the BRACES model and indicates that the total process is integrated and functions as a whole over time. What holds the total together is the activity of the case manager, an activity which—as presented—requires a diversity and complexity of roles.

## CONCLUSION

The direct practice of social work involves activities which extend well beyond in-person therapeutic interventions with clients. When examined from this perspective, it becomes important to consider the many ways in which clients' sexuality may be influenced, other than through direct efforts at the clinical level of intervention or at the system development and maintenance levels. Some informal reports by MSW students over a number of years which have provided information about the daily activities of social work practitioners in one community, have indicated that the major portion of most social worker's days is not spent in direct contact with clients. Rather, the major portion of time is spent in the other system-maintenance and linkage activities which are necessary to the provision of even the basic health and welfare services required in contemporary society (Lister, Note 6).

Consequently, social workers need to remain cognizant of the various opportunities, which could otherwise be overlooked, for positively impacting on clients' sexuality through interventions on their behalf in already impinging systems or in the resource systems to which they may otherwise be linked. If social workers do maintain this focus, then there will remain some guarantees that the sexuality of patients will be protected and enhanced and the quality of patients' lives will remain a primary concern in the provision of health care services.

## REFERENCE NOTES

1. *Webster's New Collegiate Dictionary,* Springfield, Massachusetts: 1977, p. 132.
2. Acevedo, J., Health Educator, State of Hawaii V. D. Clinic, Honolulu, Hawaii, personal communication, April, 1983.
3. Schiavi, P.C., Sexuality and Medical Illness: Specific Reference to Diabetes Mellitus, in R. Green (Ed.), *Human Sexuality, a Health Practitioner's Text,* Baltimore: William and Wilkins, 1979, p. 211.
4. *Ibid.*
5. McGowan, B.G., The Case Advocacy Function in Child Welfare Practice, *Child Welfare,* 1978, *5,* p. 282.
6. Lister, L. unpublished information from MSW students, University of Hawaii School of Social Work, Honolulu, Hawaii, 1982.

## REFERENCES

Benjamin, M., Emerging Patterns of Case Management Activities in Mental Health Settings. *Access,* Texas: University of Texas at Austin, n.d.
Bertsche, A.V., Horejsi, C.R., Coordination of Client Services. *Social Work,* 1980, *2,* 94-98.
Chandler, S., Mediation: A New Skill for Social Workers. Paper presented at the Council of Social Work Education Annual Program Meeting, Texas: Ft. Worth, March, 1983.
Cohen, H., *You Can Negotiate Anything.* Secaucus, New Jersey: Lyle Stuart, Inc., 1980.
Conte, J. & Berliner, L., Sexual Abuse of Children: Implications for Practice. *Social Casework,* 1981, *10,* 601-606.
Hardgrove, G., An Interagency Service Network to Meet Needs of Rape Victims. *Social Casework,* 1976, *4,* 245-253.
Johnson, P.J. & Rubin, A., Case Management in Mental Health: A Social Work Domain? *Social Work,* 1983, *1,* 49-55.
Maluccio, A.N. & Marlow, W.D., The Case for the Contract. *Social Work,* 1974, *1,* 28-36.
Masters, W.H. & Johnson, V.E., *Human Sexual Response,* Boston: Little, Brown and Co., 1966.
McGowan, B.G., The Case Advocacy Function in Child Welfare Practice. *Child Welfare,* 1978, *5,* 275-284.

Morris, J.N., Chave, S.P.W., Adam, C., Sirey, C., Epstein, L. & Sheehan, D.J., Vigorous Exercize in Leisure Time and the Incidence of Coronary Heart Disease. *Lancet*, 1973, *17*, 333-339.

Schiavi, P.C., Sexuality and Medical Illness: Specific Reference to Diabetes Mellitus, in R. Green (Ed.), *Human Sexuality, a Health Practitioner's Text*, Baltimore: William and Wilkins, 1979.

Sosin, M. & Caulum, S., Advocacy: A Conceptualization for Social Work Practice. *Social Work*, 1983, *1*, 12-17.

Takamura, J., Bermosk, L. & Stringfellow, L., *Health Team Development Program.* Hawaii: John A. Burns School of Medicine, 1979.

Wagner, N. & Sivarajan, E.S., Sexual Activity and the Cardiac Patient, in R. Green, (Ed.), *Human Sexuality, a Health Practitioner's Text*, Baltimore: William and Wilkins, 1979.

Wood, R. & Rose, K., Penile Implants for Impotence. *American Journal of Nursing*, 1978, *2*.

Woods, N.F., *Human Sexuality in Health and Illness*. St. Louis: C.V. Mosby Co., 1975.

# Assessing Sexual Concerns
## of Clients with
## Health Problems

James Gripton, DSW
Mary Valentich, PhD

**ABSTRACT.** Sexual counseling of clients with health problems which interfere with desired sexual expression is gaining momentum. This article examines one phase of the social work helping process-assessment when information is sought which will guide social work activities. The interaction of sex, impairment, disability and handicap is examined, and a classification of the various ways disability adversely affects aspects of sexuality is presented. Basic components of the assessment process are discussed, as well as considerations of timing and guidelines for assessment interviewing.

During the past decade health care professionals have become more aware that persons with physical illnesses and disabilities are not asexual: they have sexual desires, questions and concerns (Robinault, 1978). They may lessen the frequency or even discontinue previous sexual activities; or they may pursue their sexual goals despite physical limitations and restrictive institutional conditions (Woods, 1979, p. 281). This awareness has prompted social workers to act as advocates on behalf of those whose rights to responsible sexual expression have been infringed (Gochros and Gochros, 1977). There has also been discussion of the counseling services which may be offered to persons who are disabled to help them realize their sexual goals (Jehu, 1981; Gripton and Valentich, 1981). This article examines the initial phase of social work intervention—the assessment—when information is sought to guide social work activities in relation to client goals. The topics discussed include the rationale for social work intervention; the interaction of sex, impairment, disability and handicap; components of the assessment; timing, opportunities and conditions; and guidelines for interviewing.

## RATIONALE FOR SOCIAL WORK INTERVENTION

Social workers in health care systems are charged with maintaining a perspective on social role performance (Black, Morrison, Snyder & Tally, 1977; Caputi, 1982). Health concerns are viewed in terms of how they affect the individual's fulfillment of role expectations in the family, work, school, and other social contexts. One component of social role performance is the maintenance of satisfying sexual activities and relationships.

Sexual concerns of the patient are not a central focus of any health care profession, and none has an exclusive or preemptive mandate (Miller, Szasz and Anderson, 1981). Ideally a patient might choose any member of the health team as a sexual counselor in the expectation that all team members were skilled in sex counseling and other team members would support the patient's choice (Semmler and Semmler, 1974). In reality, physicians and nurses have been reluctant to deal with patients' sexual concerns (Friedman, 1978, p. 376; Woods, 1979, p. 107), in order to protect themselves against accusations of unethical behavior. Because physicians and nurses have intimate physical contact with patients for medical reasons, they have avoided potential embarrassment of all concerned by desexualizing the experience of physical touching (Woods, 1978, pp. 273-274 and 282-283). Indeed, the entire health care experience is generally neutered (Woods, 1978, pp. 272-286).

Social workers have assumed some responsibility for ameliorating the dehumanizing aspects of hospitals and other health care facilities (Caputi, 1982, p. 10). Further, social workers do not generally engage in physical contact with patients. Consequently they may be more comfortable than other health care personnel in dealing with patients' sexual concerns.

## INTERACTION OF SEX, IMPAIRMENT, DISABILITY, AND HANDICAP

Impairment refers to the organic component of injury or disease process. Disability is the limitation of function imposed by the impairment, and the individual's psychological reaction to it. Handicap is the social component, the manner and degree that the primary impairment and the functional disability limit the performance of social roles (Susser and Watson, 1971, pp. 357-361). These distinctions among impairment, disability and handicap are illustrated in Table 1.

Table 1: Examples of Impairment, Sexual Disability and

Sexual Handicap

| Impairment | Sexual Disability | Sexual Handicap |
|---|---|---|
| Arterio-sclerotic heart disease | Tachycardia and anginal pain with intercourse leading to anxiety and erectile difficulties | Offensive sexual overtures and comments made by male patients to women friends and employees |
| Diabetes | Erectile difficulties in men or loss of orgasmic response in women and depression | Loss of interest and avoidance of sex with partner |
| Blindness | Loss of important sensory capacity in sexual communication and arousal and feelings of despair | Unassertiveness, fear and anxiety in initiating and responding to sexual overtures |
| Low sperm count | Inability to impregnate and loss of sexual self-esteem | Resentment at inability to fulfil reproductive role |

Sexual concerns center in those components of illness or injury and its treatment that adversely affect physical performance and sensual experience, the cognitive and emotional aspects of sex, the performance of sex roles, or sexual relationships.

Figure 1 represents the person with impairment as a circle surrounded by a set of concentric rings. The circle is the individual's physical self. This is comprised of the perception of the body and its attributes, the totality of bodily sensations, and the meaning and value that the individual assigns to them. The sexual physical self is how the individual perceives and evaluates the body as a sexual instrument and object. This is shown as a segment of the physical self ring.

Disability may lead the individual to question his or her masculinity or femininity—the set of ideas that a person has about himself or herself as man or woman. If the person experiences doubts about his or her self as a sexual person, then it is sexual identity that is imperiled. Sexual identity is shown as a segment of the ring representing gender identity.

Disability may also affect how the individual performs his or her gender role—how he or she meets society's expectations that derive from being a man or woman. Again, the sexual role as a component

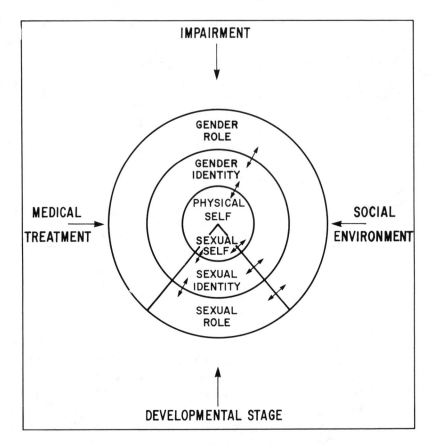

of gender role is shown as a segment of the ring that represents gender role.

The following example is used to illustrate how disability can affect the physical self, gender identity, sexual identity, gender role and sexual role. A woman who has been severely burned may be left with painful physical sensations in areas previously pleasurable to touch. Facial scars may cause her to see herself as less feminine and to question her attractiveness as a sexual person. These insecurities about gender identity and sexual identity may interfere with her sexual relationships with her partner and leave her wondering whether she will be able to meet the gender role expectations of spouse or parent.

There are four factors that shape the individual's general and sexual adjustment, and these are represented by the boundaries of the square that surrounds the rings. These are the impairment itself, medical treatment, the stage of development of the individual, and the individual's social environment. An accurate understanding of the individual's impairment, and how this disables the person in relation to sexual and other functions, is an indispensable component of the assessment. For example, the person with a relatively stable disabling condition is in a different situation than the person who has a deteriorating physical condition with a concomitant loss in sexual function. While a progressive condition provides the person with time to make adjustments to the disability, there may be an ongoing sense of grief which interferes with maintaining a satisfying sexual life. Knowledge of the current situation and prognosis are both important. Assessment is complicated by the fact that the effects on physical sexual functioning of many illnesses and injuries are highly variable and often not well understood. Furthermore, the individual's psychological reactions to the impairment, whether or not it affects the structure or functions of the sexual organs, may affect sexual expression and adjustment more profoundly than the impairment itself.

In addition to the impairment, medical treatment may also have adverse consequences. Certain medications may alter the level of sexual interest or impair specific aspects of sexual function (Kaplan, 1974, pp. 86-103). Wearing a brace or some other aspect of a treatment regimen may diminish sexual self-esteem.

The person's age when impairment occurred and the current stage of development are important considerations in assessment. Early impairment often implies restricted opportunities for sexual development and gratification. For those whose impairment occurred at a later stage, the trauma of the sexual disability will relate to the sexual developmental tasks in which they were engaged at that time. In the case of males with diabetes, the man whose erectile difficulties begin at 60 is not dealing with the same concerns as the man whose erectile difficulties began at 30.

The fourth factor is the social environment of the person with a disability. It is this that determines the handicap—the way in which the impairment adversely affects the performance of social roles. The most critical aspect of the social environment is the availability of a sexual partner. The person without a partner may be despondent about being able to find one, and the nature of the disability may indeed make this a frustrating search. Some persons with a lifelong disability may never have experienced a physical sexual relationship, and the nature of their disability may effectively preclude that possibility.

The person with a disability whose partner disqualifies him or her as a sexual person because of the disability may be worse off than one without a partner. A supportive partner, however, can help the disabled person to overcome feelings of being unworthy of another's love or sexual attention.

Gochros and Gochros (1977, p. xx) have noted that the only sexual activity that receives general and unqualified approval in our society is that which can result in a socially approved pregnancy. This attitude is labeled the reproductive bias. Consequently, the person with an impairment, especially if it is visible, is at risk of being disqualified as a sexual person by family, friends, neighbours, and work colleagues. Those confined to an institution are especially vulnerable to sexual oppression.

The following is a comprehensive classification of the ways in which impairment, disability, medical treatment, and the individual's developmental stage and social environment may adversely affect sexual experience or performance.

1. Adverse effects on physical sexual peformance.

—Effects on structure and/or function of the genital system.
—Effects on level or stability of sexual interest.
—Impediments to sexual communication, verbal or non-verbal.
—Restrictions on sexual repertoire because of amputation, lack of ambulation or coordination.
—Loss of sensory response to sexual stimuli.
—Effects on reproductive capacity.
—Effects on contraception.

2. Adverse effects on psychosexual development, experience and satisfaction.

—Inaccurate and/or inadequate understanding of the implications of impairment for current and prospective sexual performance and experience.
   • Client may have unfounded fears that continuation of sexual activity will aggravate impairment or disability, or will be fatal.

—Adverse effects of impairment or disability on sexual self-image.

- Client may consider self inadequate as a sexual person because he or she cannot meet performance norms or suffers from loss of sexual sensation.
- Client may view self as an inadequate sexual person or abnormal because of the belief that persons with his or her particular impairment or disability should not be interested in sex. This may lead to denial of sexual interests.
- Client may consider self an inadequate sexual person because impairment or disability is considered to have reduced sexual attractiveness. The impairment or disability may have led the client to adopt a negative or distorted body image.
- Client may attempt to maintain an adequate sexual self-image by denying limitations imposed by disability on sexual performance. Inadequate sexual self-image may contribute to lowered self-esteem.
- Impairment or disability may create problems of personal hygiene that may undermine a client's positive sexual self-image.

3. Adverse effects on gender identity.

—Gender identity is threatened because of inability to perform certain aspects of the normative gender role, and this in turn affects sense of self as an adequate sexual person.
—Gender identity is threatened because normative sexual performance or appearance is viewed as a necessary condition of masculinity or femininity.

4. Adverse social effects, or handicap.

—Sexual oppression through social attitudes that negate the sexuality and/or restrict the sexual expression of persons suffering from the client's impairment or disability.
—Negative attitudes or responses of partners to client's sexuality.
—Negative attitudes or responses of other significant persons in the life of the client, including health care givers, to the client's sexuality.
—Obstacles to communication about sex imposed by anxieties,

fears, distaste or disapproval evoked from others by the client's impairment or disability. These inhibiting feelings or attitudes may be toward the impairment or the disability itself, or toward the continuing sexual interests of the client.

## COMPONENTS OF A SEXUAL ASSESSMENT

The focus of the sexual assessment of persons with disabilities derives from the general goals of counselling that apply to such clients. These are:

1. To help clients gain a realistic perception of the disabling effect of impairments on physical sexual performance;
2. To help clients explore and evaluate their potential for sexual satisfaction;
3. To help clients deal effectively with strains in sexual relationships resulting from the disability;
4. To help minimize handicap by asserting their sexual rights with persons or organizations that deny them.

The assessment process will vary in relation to the social worker's theoretical orientation, the organizational mandate for sex counseling, available resources, and the client's accessibility to and desire for counseling. The major components, nonetheless, include: the client's sexual concerns; current sexual functioning; duration of the problem; changes in sexual functioning; sexual development history; client's efforts to resolve the problem; medical evaluation of the impairment; and goal formulation.

A client's sexual concerns may relate to any aspect of the individual depicted in Figure 1. In treating approximately 400 acute spinal cord injured persons and over 200 persons with various illnesses and disabilities, Miller et al. (1981) note that the three most common sexual concerns are physiologically based:

"Will I be able to satisfy my partner?" (i.e., will there be an erection, will there be a receptive vagina); "Will I be able to have satisfaction?" (i.e., will there be normal sensations, orgasm, etc.) and "Will I be able to have children?" (i.e., will there be ejaculation, normal sperm, ovulation, required hormone levels, etc.). (pp. 5-6)

The client's sexual concerns suggest what the client would like to change. These desired changes, specified in behavioral terms, become the goals of the helping process.

Information on the client's current sexual functioning includes sexual interests, desires, fantasies, activities and opportunities. Health care personnel in close contact with the patient, as well as partners, can contribute significantly in this regard. It is important that the information gained by observation or interview be specific. A useful technique is to ask the client, or client and partner, to describe in a step-by-step fashion a recent sexual encounter. Who did what, when, and for how long, what did each person think and feel as this was happening, and how did they perceive their partner's reactions? As in sex therapy, an evaluation of the couple's interpersonal relationship is critical in order to gauge the resources available for problem resolution (Lobitz and Lobitz, 1978, p. 97).

A wide range of measurements of sexual knowledge, attitudes, values, fears, and experiences are available. These can facilitate assessment, measurement of client change, and evaluation of counseling effectiveness. They should be used selectively with clients with disabilities, however, since they have been developed and standardized with non-disabled subjects, and many are intercourse focused.

Information on the client's current sexual functioning is complete when there has been a medical evaluation of the implications of the impairment for sexual performance. Woods (1978, pp. 84-89) describes how health professionals can sensitively gather this kind of information.

It is important to establish the duration of the problem and events in the client's life that may bear on the development of the problem. It must not be assumed, however, that the client's present sexual concerns originated in the disability; or that they can be entirely explained by it.

In ascertaining what changes have occurred in sexual function, information will be obtained on the history of the problem (Woods, 1978, p. 80; Annon, 1974), and on the client's sexual development. The sexual development history includes the following:

- earliest sensual and sexual experiences;
- childhood sex play;
- adolescent sexual experience;
- self-stimulation history;

- sex fantasies over time;
- learning about sex;
- family attitudes regarding sensuality and sexuality;
- development of gender and sexual identities;
- development of gender and sex roles;
- identification of sexual orientation;
- other and same sex encounters and relationships, past and present.

The sexual history helps explain why the client acquired or is experiencing the current problem and what is maintaining it (Lobitz and Lobitz, 1978, p. 94). If a partner is available, a sex history will also be obtained. There are guides for obtaining such information in the sex therapy literature (LoPiccolo and Heiman, 1978; Masters and Johnson, 1970).

Several incidental therapeutic benefits occur in the process of obtaining the history. Clients have the opportunity to ask questions and express fears. They gain useful information, and have their sexuality affirmed despite their impairment and disability. They may become more hopeful about the possibility of improving their sexual life. Hence, through the client's response to the assessment process itself, the social worker will gain important clues about the client's desire for change, capacity for sustained effort, and the kinds of intervention that may prove successful. The social worker, in interpreting the purpose and nature of the assessment, will also explain the nature of social work intervention and discuss the client's expectations of the helping process.

## TIMING, OPPORTUNITIES, AND CONDITIONS

The assessment process has three phases: initial contact, exploration, and formulation of intervention goals. The initial contact phase begins whenever the social worker first meets the client. The social worker, in explaining his or her role, should refer to the possibility of the client having sexual concerns and describe the services that are available. The social worker's comfortable introduction of the topic both validates the individual as a sexual person and gives permission for sexual concerns to be raised when the client chooses to do so. The risk of embarrassing the client by this initiative is far outweighed by the risk that the client will otherwise be denied help in relation to an important aspect of his or her disability.

If the client agrees to work with the social worker in relation to sexual concerns, the exploration phase of the assessment begins. The opportunities to talk with the client may be formally planned or arise spontaneously. Much depends on the setting, the privacy that is available, and the access the social worker has to the client. A client who has not asked for help or acknowledged significant sexual concerns cannot be expected to participate in the assessment. Clients may also hesitate to provide sexual information because of concerns about how such information will be used. Sexuality is one of the most private aspects of ourselves. On the first occasion that it is discussed, clients should be told why the information sought is needed, with whom it will be shared, where it will be recorded, and how confidentiality will be protected. This issue has particular implications for multi-disciplinary settings. Ground rules should be established concerning responsibility for initiating discussion of sexuality, explaining what help is available, providing counseling, and making referrals to other team members. The client must be protected from being asked independently and unsystematically by various team members about sexual concerns.

Goal specification marks the culmination of the exploration of client concerns and the development by client and social worker of a shared understanding of the dynamics of the problem. The assessment statement prepared by the worker becomes the basis for intervention by the social worker or other team members, or for a referral.

## GUIDELINES FOR INTERVIEWING

The general principles and procedures for effective interviewing (Fischer, 1978, p. 251) also apply to the assessment of sexual concerns of persons with disabilities. The following guidelines identify those that have particular reference to sexual assessment. While the occasional client may have several health care professionals raising the question of sexual concerns, it is more likely that no one has introduced the topic. Some clients will take the initiative themselves, but most will not. While it is important to introduce the topic early, one should be sensitive to both individual and group differences in discussing sexual matters. Women tend to be less assertive than men in presenting their sexual concerns, and men have more difficulty in discussing their feelings about sex. Furthermore, there are differences among cultures concerning reticence about sexual matters. Often clients express a preference for a male or female social worker. The gender of the social worker is probably a more important consideration in sex counseling than in counseling for other concerns. Recognition that most people feel anxiety around talking about sex is helpful, as is identification of sexual concerns that are common to persons with their disability.

Because many people are unskilled in talking about sex, modelling of clear and comfortable communication by the social worker is helpful. Good communication in the interview involves building a common sex vocabulary with the client. Such vocabularies are developed through a trial and error process during the assessment phase, and will often consist of a mix of medical terms and slang. A sex-oppressive cultural tradition has denied us a sexual vulgate—a widely understood, emotionally neutral and reasonably precise sexual vocabulary. Medical/scientific terminology has the advantage of precision, but the disadvantage that it is impersonal, occasionally pejorative, and often misunderstood. It is the vocabulary that the social worker may favor and that many clients may expect. Some clients will be more comfortable with slang, but it is imprecise, repugnant to some, and also misunderstood. The social worker should convey acceptance of the client's vocabulary, primarily by not registering discomfort; and by using the client's terms. If the client's vocabulary is ambiguous or imprecise, then it may be necessary to introduce and explain alternative terms. Social workers are unlikely to develop skills in sexual communication without special training involving desensitization and role playing practice.

With non-verbal clients, the social worker may use other media such as paper and pencil, blackboards, word cards, pictures, films, dolls with genitals, or models of genitals.

When a partner participates in the assessment, it should be kept in mind that the couple may not have shared their sexual histories with each other, or may be apprehensive about what the partner has said about their sexual relationship in separate interviews.

Some clients with a disability demonstrate their sexual nature by touching the social worker or by suggestive sexual talk or display. The social worker should convey how he or she feels when the client behaves in this way, and by discussing what the client is trying to convey. The social worker's response should affirm the client's right to be a sexual person, but the social worker must also assert his or her expectation to be viewed as a helping professional and not as a potential sexual partner. Effective affirmation of the client's sexuality depends on how the social worker answers the client's question, asked directly, obliquely, or implied: "Am I attractive, interesting and sexual? And not in a general way, but to you?" It is important for the client to hear:

> Yes, you are a sexual person! You have every right to search for satisfying ways to express your sexuality. This may or may not involve sexual partners. None of this is diminished by the fact that I am not able to be your sexual partner. The important point is that it is possible for others to be interested in you, both as a person and as a sexual partner.

Occasionally clients will ask about the social worker's sexual life. The social worker should consider disclosing if this facilitates client sharing or if it validates the client's own sexuality, but the social worker should not feel obliged to provide such information.

## REFERENCES

Annon, J. *The behavioral treatment of sexual problems.* Honolulu: Enabling Systems, 1974.

Black, D., Morrison, J., Snyder, L. & Tally, P. Model for clinical social work practice in a health care facility. *Social Work in Health Care.* 1977, 3(2), 143-148.

Caputi, M. A 'quality of life' model for social work practice in health care. *Health and Social Work.* 1982, 7(2), 103-110.

Fischer, J. *Effective casework practice: An eclectic approach.* New York: McGraw-Hill, 1978.

Friedman, J. *Sexual adjustment of the postcoronary male.* In J. LoPiccolo & L. LoPiccolo (Eds.), *Handbook of sex therapy.* New York: Plenum Press, 1978.

Gochros, H. & Gochros, J. (Eds.). *The sexually oppressed.* New York: Association Press, 1977.

Gripton, J. & Valentich, M. Sex counselling of clients with physical illnesses and disabilities. In D. Freeman & B. Trute (Eds.), *Treating families with special needs.* Ottawa: Alberta Association of Social Workers & Canadian Association of Social Workers, 1981.

Jehu, D. Implications of physical disability for sexual function and rehabilitation. In D. Freeman & B. Trute (Eds.), *Treating families with special needs.* Ottawa: Alberta Association of Social Workers & Canadian Association of Social Workers, 1981.

Kaplan, H. *The new sex therapy.* New York: Brunner-Mazel, 1974.

Lobitz, W. C. & Lobitz, G. Clinical assessment in the treatment of sexual dysfunctions. In J. LoPiccolo & L. LoPiccolo (Eds.), *Handbook of sex therapy.* New York: Plenum Press, 1981.

LoPiccolo, L. & Heiman, J. Sexual assessment and history interview. In J. LoPiccolo and L. LoPiccolo (Eds.), *Handbook of sex therapy.* New York: Plenum Press, 1978.

Masters, W & Johnson, V. *Human Sexual Inadequacy.* Boston: Little, Brown, 1970.

Miller, S., Szasz, G. & Anderson, L. *Sexual health care clinician in an acute spinal cord injury unit.* Archives of Physical Medicine and Rehabilitation. 1981, 62, 315-320.

Robinault, I. P. *Sex, society and the disabled.* New York: Harper & Row, 1978.

Semmler, C. & Semmler, M. Counselling the coronary patient. *American Journal of Occupational Therapy,* 1974, 28(10), 609.

Susser, N.W. & Watson, W. *Sociology in Medicine* (2nd ed.). London: Oxford University Press, 1971.

Woods, N. Adaptation to hospitalization and illness. In N. Woods, *Human sexuality in health and illness.* Toronto: C.V. Mosby, 1979.

Woods, N. & Mandetta, A. Preventive intervention. In N. Woods, *Human sexuality in health and illness.* Toronto: C. V. Mosby, 1979.

# Sexuality and Chronic Illness

Mary S. Sheridan, ACSW

**ABSTRACT.** Chronic illness has numerous sexual implications. Threat to bodily integrity, a self-concept as "different," and interaction with gender role all have their effect on sexual functioning. In addition, diseases such as hypertension, diabetes, and renal failure are associated with specific sexual threats or dysfunctions. Problems may come from the disease process itself, from medication or treatment side-effects, or from the psychosomatic interaction. Therapy should be directed at the whole patient and include the partner. A problem-solving approach is useful, combined with focus on gender and sensuality as distinct from genital performance. Throughout counseling, the worker must be sensitive to the delicacy of these issues and to the client's ethical choices.

Sexuality is far less important in chronic illness than continuity of the person as a whole. But sexuality involves a delicate balance between mind and body. When this balance is disturbed, as it is in illness, sexuality is affected. And because both physician and patient are often reticent to discuss sexuality, it tends to be lost behind considerations of survival.

This is unfortunate. The implications of gender and sexuality are not lost when one becomes ill. Just as patients worry about how illness will affect occupation, diet, or longevity, so they are concerned for their sexuality. This has always been recognized implicitly. Get well cards reveal an abundance of buxom nurses, panting male patients, and revealing hospital gowns. Popular books and films about health professionals depict "superhealers," but also show the young doctors and nurses seizing every opportunity for intimacy. There is an assumption, as in the days when no decent woman became a nurse, that knowledge of bodily processes leads to sexual activity.

The strength of these themes in popular culture demonstrates the strength of the threat.

Thus the male patient enters the hospital with a number of preconscious notions. He fears, and may symbolically experience, loss of his masculinity and adulthood. Stripped of belongings and privacy, wheeled from place to place, invaded by tubes and instruments, he is placed at the day-to-day mercy of women. He may fear both responding to them sexually and not responding. He may also feel compromised by taking directions from a male physician or nurse. Already tending to regress in response to the impact of illness, he may see his choices as childlike submission or adolescent rebellion.

On the surface, things are easier for the female patient. Raised to submit to the authority of the male, she is also comforted by the care of the female. Women tend to take charge of the health of the family, and thus they are more familiar with medical rituals. But if males are tempted to reject care, and thus be under-treated, females are tempted to over-dependence and thus may be exploited.[1] We are gradually becoming aware of the sexist aspects of medicine as they affect both men and women. Consumer-oriented care, with the patient taking responsibility for final decision-making, offers a solution. Such an approach reminds patients that they purchase health care just as they do other professional services. Thus they may choose the amount of dependency they wish, and free the practitioner from demands to be a perfect parent. Such care, however, requires attitudes which are foreign, not only to many patients, but to many health professionals as well.

Beyond the ethos of illness, however, are specific impacts on gender and genital function. For the acutely ill there is likely to be a reasonably quick return to premorbid functioning. Some patients will be particularly vulnerable to the effects of illness; they may suffer a longer sense of impairment, or may find that the illness contains a growth-inducing message. But for the chronically ill, or the person whose acute episode is the beginning of a chronic process, a new identity must be incorporated. Intensely personal questions must be answered: what place will the illness have in the patient's life, how does it relate to the patient's beliefs and values, how will it affect plans and relationships? These issues include questions of gender role and sexuality. The answers come only slowly, from an interaction of personality factors, the nature of the disease, and the help available to the patient.

## GENERAL SEXUAL EFFECTS OF ILLNESS

There are both general and specific ways in which chronic illness affects sexuality (see Table I). All chronic diseases affect self-concept, though their specific effect will vary with the type of disease. Cole and Cole [2] identify four "types" in the illness experience, based on variables of age of onset and the progressiveness of the disease. "Type I" illness begins early in life and is non-progressive. Cere-

TABLE I

IMPACT OF ILLNESS ON SEXUALITY

I. Changes in body image and self-concept

  A. Due to diagnosis

    1. Timing in the life cycle

    2. Implications for present and future

  B. Due to treatment

    1. Medical, such as drugs and radiation

    2. Surgical

  C. Due to other connotations of illness

    1. Associations with aging

    2. Associations with weakness, unhealthiness

    3. No longer a "real" man or woman

II. Changes in role functioning

  A. Increased dependence

  B. Role loss

  C. Role reversal or transfer

III. Depression

IV. Changes in relationship with partner

V. Pain

VI. Total demands of coping with illness

VII. Specific effects on sexual performance

  A. Associated with particular diseases

  B. Associated with particular treatments

  C. Increased fear or embarrassment

  D. Reproductive issues

bral palsy or post-traumatic amputation would be examples. Type I patients always feel different, and are so perceived by others. Because of lingering prejudices, they may not receive adequate sex education. Many around them believe that they will be unable to participate in adult sexual behavior, particularly where the disability is severe. They may come to believe this of themselves.

"Type II" patients have progressive diseases with early onset. They may have muscular dystrophy or cystic fibrosis, for example. They must also integrate feelings of being different, which are exacerbated by the fact that they are always "sickly" and expecting or experiencing deterioration. They, too, may assume that they will never be intimate with another person, and may also have to deal with limited fertility or ability to engage in intercourse.

"Type III" patients have adult-onset impairments which are stable, such as accidental losses. They will be able to use the sexual roles and relationships already established in their adjustment to the new illness. For the majority, rehabilitation will involve the restoration of function through adaptive technqiues, education, physical therapy, and counseling. The quality of the pre-morbid adjustment will determine the complications which arise.

"Type IV" patients have adult-onset progressive disease; the majority of chronic illnesses are in this category. Such patients can also use pre-morbid adjustment to facilitate rehabilitation, but because the course of the illness is constantly changing, adaptation is an ongoing task. They have less opportunity for planning, and more scope for depression. They may also have undergone a period of deterioration prior to diagnosis, and can thus present with sexual problems which they have attributed to personal failure rather than to disease. Impotence or repeated vaginal infection, for example, can be clues to diabetes. Such areas must be explored and patients be given an opportunity to correct misconceptions.

Of course the exact developmental stage, whether of childhood or adult life, will have its implications on adjustment to illness. The specific meaning and implications of the disease, as they interact with what the person values, make every patient's experience of illness different. Cancer, for example, is often erroneously believed to be a death sentence. A heart attack might seem to be a warning to slow down. Strokes are frequently portrayed in literature as the outcome (punishment?) of anger.

The treatment prescribed for the illness will also have effects on bodily image. Patients maintained on steroid drugs, for example, gain weight, while dialysis patients tend to lose muscle mass. Certain anti-cancer drugs cause a loss of hair, and radiation treatments may cause atrophy or scarring. The loss of any organ will be experienced as a loss to the self as a whole. Where there is surgical loss to any of the organs associated with reproduction or sexuality, particularly if there is a loss of desired fertility or function, this is central to sexual self-concept. Even the smallest of orthopedic appliances erects a barrier to interaction with the world, or becomes the focus of that interaction. All of these factors will impinge on one's sense of wholeness and attractiveness.

There are other connotations to the diagnosis of chronic illness. The discovery of a bodily betrayal may be one's first real confrontation with aging and mortality. Arthritis and other conditions which affect the ease and range of movement are clearly associated with old age. And aging, as is well known, is culturally associated with asexuality.

Sex is not only associated with youth, but with strength, health, and competence. Society also dichotomizes people into healthy ("normal") and unhealthy ("abnormal"), reserving sex for the former. The reservation and the dichotomy are both wrong, since the majority of adults are not in perfect health but are sexually active. However, it may be difficult for the more seriously or visibly ill to believe themselves capable of sex.

One's definition of a "real" man or woman is personal, but derived from cultural and subcultural norms. For many patients, gender identity is not "real" unless it includes reproductive capacity or genital wholeness. Thus the loss of a breast or testicle may be seen as the loss of gender identity. Hysterectomy or vasectomy may also compromise sexual identity. Feelings about such a loss may be introjected on the self or projected onto the partner. It is worth remembering also that in our culture womanhood tends to be ascribed, while manhood is achieved. Thus each sex will experience loss in a different way.

Illness often forces changes in role behaviors, and roles are still strongly sex-linked. Most sick people must increase dependence—on health professionals, family members, or medications. Such dependence is traditionally the province of women, though American society has a strong value on independence for both sexes. For many patients illness involves a loss, perhaps of occupation or perhaps of the ability to participate fully in a favorite sport or hobby. There may be both positive and negative aspects to such loss. Patients may themselves question whether secondary gain is contributing to their symptoms, and family members may also believe that the disability is a way of avoiding unwanted social or occupational responsibilities. Such use of a real condition (which is much more common than the "manufacture" of a psychogenic condition) is not uncommon, since illness is accepted almost universally as a method of avoidance. However it is extremely difficult to untangle the strands of psychological and physical processes present in any illness.

When one member of a couple is disabled, role reversal may take place. This is usually seen in the form of the wife assuming responsibilities of family support which were previously the province of the now-disabled male. Often the true situation could be called role transfer, since the husband may be unwilling to take on home responsibilities (which he conceptualizes as female and therefore final proof of his emasculation.) Thus the wife has a double burden and may even be criticized for contributing to her husband's loss of self esteem. Such situations potentiate identity loss, anger, and tension in both partners.

A brief review of the effects of illness so far reveals much potential for growth, but little that could be seen in positive terms. Helplessness, loss of role and bodily function, anger, and impaired hopes for the future are easily recognized as triggers to depression. When one feels sick in addition to this, and perhaps receives medications with a depressant effect, it is not surprising that depression is the result. This depression, in turn, affects self image, sexual functioning, and intimate relationships.

Pain also contributes to depression and to the total impact of illness on the patient. Although everyone experiences pain, we understand little about it. It is clear that men are supposed to be stoic, and that women are expected to show suffering more. There are aspects of pain which are romantic, mystical, religious, and erotic.

Pain may be an incidental part of the illness, or the major disabling effect. Men and women in pain are treated differently by health professionals; in a British hospital study men's requests for pain medication were refused while women were offered analgesics.[3] Chronic pain is wearing; it makes each activity more difficult; it makes the person appear older and less attractive. It is totally subjective, and thus a focus for real or imputed psychological processes. The fear of pain or inflicting it cannot but inhibit activities aimed at pleasure.

Chronic illness demands adaptation in a relationship. The marriage service asks fidelity "in sickness and in health," but this is only a hypothetical promise for most couples. The relationship must absorb new financial strains with often diminished resources, and the healthy partner often finds new restrictions on ability to plan, on time, and on activity. Just as both partners bring to a relationship different concepts of what it means to be a wife or husband, so will they carry—often unconsciously and for years—notions of what it means to be spouse of a sick person. When these ideas diverge at such an emotionally vulnerable time the hurts may go deep. The healthy partner may have needs, emotional or physical, which the sick partner cannot meet, the illness itself may complicate the equation, or both partners may have problems of illness. One can easily imagine the problems associated with a heavily sedated wife who loses track of time and does not realize her husband is visiting, or the husband who misinterprets his wife's need for reassurance and believes she has fallen in love with his doctor.

The experience of coping with chronic illness must be seen in its totality, which will be more than the sum of its parts. The sexual arena will be a place in which this whole experience may be acted out, so that problems more related to illness may appear to be sexual problems. At the same time, however, intimacy may be an area in which bonds with one's partner can be reaffirmed, in which the sick person may be a source of gratification and reassurance to the well partner, and in which healing may begin.

## THE SPECIFIC SEXUAL IMPACT OF ILLNESS

There are a number of illnesses which are associated with impingement of sexual performance, though the extent is variable for individual patients. Many patients with heart disease, particularly after heart attack, fear sexual activity. Statistically there is a decrease in sexual activity after heart attack, for reasons that are unclear.[4] Exercise studies have demonstrated that the majority of patients can begin or resume sexual activity if they are capable of climbing several flights of stairs. (Some patients do develop arrhythmia specific to sexual activity.) For most patients, a rehabilitative program in which sexual activity is resumed just as physical activity is resumed will be appropriate. Marital intercourse appears to be less taxing to the heart than extramarital liaisons.

Chronic renal failure is frequently accompanied by loss of sexual ability or interest. Diabetes and hypertension, two diseases which may exist independently or predispose to renal failure, are also associated with impotence in the male and loss of orgasm in the female. The reasons are poorly understood. In the case of renal failure, there are apparently hormonal alterations which do not completely reverse even with successful transplant. Progressive neuropathy is implicated in diabetes. Medication side effects may be the principal cause in hypertension, but the relationships between hyptertension and sexuality are not well understood. Sex therapy can be tried for all these patients. If it is unsuccessful, male diabetic and renal patients may be candidates for penile implants. Hypertensive patients should be offered changes of medication until optimal blood pressure control can balance with sexual functioning. Both hypertensives and partners should be counseled that they do not have a problem in which restriction of excitement (sexual or otherwise) is curative.

Patients with chronic obstructive pulmonary disease may experience bronchospasm or shortness of breath during intercourse. They may avoid sexual activity for that reason. Asthmatics who have attacks induced by exercise may suffer similar reactions during coitus. These patients may be helped by appropriate medication, positioning, or other therapy.

Spinal cord impairments are frequently associated with sexual dysfunction, the extent depending on location and nature of the lesion. Male patients may continue to have erections, with or without ejaculation; even with ejaculation, fertility is usually impaired. Female patients experience less sensation than males, but usually retain menstruation and fertility. They need contraceptive advice sensitive to their medical condition and predicated on the assumption that they will be sexual. Spasms, incontinence, and pressure sores often are sources of practical problems or embarrassment. Some surgeries to allow bladder control or reduce pain will impair fertility in spinal cord patients.

Stroke, arthritis, and other general conditions will have an effect on sexuality because of the pervasive disability or pain which may be associated. Extensive pelvic surgery, such as that done for various forms of cancer, may result in sexual dysfunction. Physicians and surgeons are more aware today of minimizing the effects of such procedures, but some impairment may be inevitable. All patients deserve an honest appraisal, in advance where possible, of the effects of illness on sexual functioning. As part of this, they deserve to know the extent to which rehabilitation and cosmetic repair are possible.

Beyond surgery, patients may have sexual side effects from other therapeutic methods. Radiation therapy for cervical cancer, for example, may cause coital pain. A number of medications, taken for a wide variety of conditions, may have side effects which affect sexual function. Table II provides a list of the general classes of medications, with some specific compounds, which *may* be implicated in problems brought to the worker's attention. This list is intended only as a guide; not all medications in a given class are implicated, and many medications cause reactions in only a small minority of patients receiving them. Further, drug reactions are highly individual. Patients may have problems with drugs not on the list, or may attribute to drugs reactions which are more probably psychogenic.

Because sexuality is so personal, so evocative of vulnerability, sexual dysfunction is a source of worry and embarrassment. Fear of losing bowel or bladder control, of impotence, of the partner's revulsion, all inhibit sexual sharing. The patient's self confidence, as well as the stability of the relationship, will affect the extent to which sexuality is perceived as possible and desirable.

The effects of illness on reproductive capacity also affect both sexual expression and relationships. It is the context of choice which makes birth control desirable. Some of the chronically ill, such as males with cystic fibrosis, must accept the likelihood that they will never produce children of their own. Those who lose the capacity to parent may feel personally diminished, or feel that they have less to offer a partner. All have lost an important source of gratification and enhanced self esteem.

## COUNSELING ISSUES

Of necessity, the above has been brief and general. This discussion of counseling must also present only principles of wide applicability. Most social workers in general practice, even in health settings, do only limited sexual counseling. Knowing the issues and techniques is important to them, both because sexual issues are pervasive in health problems and because health problems are closely related to sexual problems. Any worker should be skilled at the differential diagnoses which will suggest referral to physician or sex therapist, or retention of the case in the worker's own practice. An

TABLE II

SEXUAL SIDE EFFECTS OF PRESCRIPTION MEDICATIONS[5]

| Drug | Changed sexual ability | Menstrual changes | Breast changes | Changed Desire | Genital Irritation | Permanent Sterility |
|---|---|---|---|---|---|---|
| Adrenocorticoids (long term)* | | X | | | | |
| Amphetamines* | | | | X | | |
| Anti-alcohol (Antabuse) | X | | | | | |
| Anti-cancer** | | X | X | | | X |
| Anti-cholesterol* | X | | | | | |
| Anticoagulant (Heparin)*** | | X | | | | |
| Antihypertensives* | X | X | X | | | |
| Anti-thyroid* | | X | | | | |
| Anti-tuberculars | X | X | X | | | |
| Appetite suppressants | X | | | X | | |
| Belladonna compounds* | X | | | | | |
| Drugs for fibrocyctic breasts or endometriosis | | X | X | | | |
| Fertility agents | | X | X | | | |
| Gastro-intestinal drugs* | X | X | X | | | |
| Hormones* | | X | X | X | | |
| Psychotropics* | X | X | X | | | |
| Vaginal anti-infectives | | | | | X | |

*Use of some drugs in this class is associated with birth defects or side effects in the newborn. For a few drugs, this is true even if the drug was discontinued months before conception.

**Birth defects are associated with use by males as well as females.

***Not associated with birth defects, but may cause bleeding problems in the new mother.

impotent male whose problems began with his antihypertensive medication should suggest an immediate course of action. In the course of a general medical practice, the treatment contract may or may not call for explicit work on sexual issues. But the worker ought to know when they are likely and how to raise appropriate questions with patients.

In dealing with sexual and gender problems of the ill, the worker will find familiar techniques and axioms helpful. The worker's comfort with sexuality, beginning where the client is, universalization, and sensitive, reflective discussion facilitate sharing. By asking questions like, "How is the sexual part of your life?"[6] or "Did you know that many people with this illness have sexual problems?" the worker suggests that sex is a normal, treatable concern. It is, of course, worthy of note that sexual dysfunction is very common in the healthy population. The disentangling of emotional and physical themes in the sexuality of the chronically ill is difficult, and should be undertaken with the approach of finding the extent to which each contributes. This is far more effective than an either/or dichotomy. Where a sexual problem is of fairly recent origin, in the context of a good relationship and not causing undue distress, it may well be treated by the non-specialist. Otherwise, referral to a sex therapist or multidisciplinary team may be more appropriate.[7]

Sexual behavior and sexual counseling are filled with philosophical, cultural, and ethical ramifications. The worker must never attempt to enforce personal values on the client, including the pervasive modern value that everyone should have genital sexual activity. French says, "the new American sin is nonsexuality, even though we haven't yet got rid of the old one, which is sexuality."[8] The worker should present a range of options, from which the client chooses those most congruent with his needs and values. Unconscious repression, not sublimation, damages. A handy rule of thumb in dealing with the chronically ill or disabled is that they have the same right to sexuality as the non-impaired. That is, the same right to information, education, expression, marriage, parenthood, or homosexuality as someone without their physical condition. This implies personal choice, not license or Puritanism. It implies that sex is a natural part of life, to be reclaimed by the patient and not given by the therapist. It is an adult-adult, and not parent-child, approach.

In counseling, it is frequently necessary to involve other health professionals. The physician speaks with a particular authority, and the worker has an obligation to facilitate the patient's relationship to the physician. Workers also have a role in reminding the physician to discuss sexuality, to offer repeated discussions over time, or to include the partner. Patients need specific information addressed to their own situation. It is unfortunate, in this regard, that so much still remains to be learned about sexuality.

Some specific counseling approaches are helpful to the patient who is trying to integrate illness and sexuality. First, the area of sexuality should be kept as broad as possible. Patients will tend to focus on specific genital activites which they may have difficulty performing. The worker should begin by differentiating between sexuality and genital function; one is not less of a man or woman because of difficulties in intercourse. The focus should be on intimacy and sensuality; every human being, whether disabled or not, has need for those. Everyone has, and can enhance, the capability of giving and receiving warmth, affection, and pleasure.

Patients thus step back from the goal of coitus, if they find it difficult, and concentrate on those things in which they find pleasure. This might mean exploration of other body areas (spinal cord patients often have enhanced sensation just above the level of impairment). Consonant with values and preferences, couples may find full gratification in manual or oral stimulation or in contact between the genitals and other parts of the body. At times the relief from stress which this approach provides will aid in the eventual reestablishment of genital sexuality.

Practical problems must often be overcome, sometimes with the aid of other health professionals. The dyspneic patient may need to change to a sitting position, take bronchodilators, or receive a prescription for oxygen by nasal cannula. The pain patient might be aided by warm baths, massage, or carefully positioned pillows. Preparation for sex, though it reduces spontaneity, may increase comfort. Incontinent patients may empty appliances and remove catheters, timing of medications may reduce discomfort, stomas may be covered—as by sexually stimulating underwear.

Healthy people use many aids to intimacy, from gauzy romantic novels to soothing oils and lotions to more explicit media and devices. Fantasy can be very important in re-establishing activity. "Aids" must be understood widely as those things which overcome problems and facilitate loving reciprocity.

For many couples a change in accustomed sexual positions will be necessary. This is difficult, especially in long relationships where certain places and gestures have been associated with pleasure, gender role, or normalcy. As a general rule, the person not in pain should accept the most weight and movement. This will often mean that the woman becomes more active. Reassurance that this is not a form of dominance will be helpful; the focus must always be on mutual pleasure so that sex does not become one more service done for the invalid.

When patients are confined to institutions, questions of sexuality become more difficult. There are frequent discussions in the literature about the need for privacy and conjugal visits in hospitals and nursing homes. Any sexual activity on the part of patients is generally resisted by staff, and it seems unlikely that this will change in the near future. Perhaps a more practical solution is to make provision for liberal pass privileges. Portable oxygen cylinders, light weight wheel chairs, and heparin locks on IVs would seem feasible for those patients at a certain level of affluence and with concerned partners. Going out on pass also allows the patient to choose activity in a privacy which a "do not disturb" sign denies. Suggesting and facilitating such passes is fully appropriate for social workers.

## *CONCLUSIONS*

Helping patients to adjust to the sexual aspects of their disease is always a process of trial and error, facilitated by sharing among patients and those who work closely with them. A well functioning interdisciplinary team probably provides optimal care of the whole patient. In its absence, the worker needs to develop a network of sensitive professionals for referral, and needs to draw upon the self help groups and health-related organizations in the community. Many of these, such as the American Cancer Society, have programs and publications specifically addressed to sexually compromised patients.

Intervention into the sexuality of another is difficult. One must neither assume nor presume. One must not trample on feelings, but one must have the courage to raise difficult issues. One must above all accept the decisions of the patient, even if that acceptance includes a hope—and perhaps its expression—that the patients may not always choose to decide in that way.

As the health care professional with special concern for the patient's emotional health, and for the health of relationships beyond the hospital, the social worker has a special place in facilitating sexual rehabilitation. The contribution of social workers to this endeavor has, no doubt, been significant. But there is still a great deal to be learned, not only about the pathophysiology of sex and illness but also about its psychological and personal effects. It is to be hoped that social workers will take their place in this search, and will not be hesitant to share what they have learned with others in the medical professions.

## NOTES

1. This subject is an extremely important one, omitted from this chapter as it is developed elsewhere in more detail.

2. T. Cole and S. Cole, "Sexual Health and Physical Disability." Chapter 15 in H. Lief, ed., *Sexual Problems in Medical Practice*. Monroe, Wisc., American Medical Association, 1981

3. M. Bond, "Personality and Pain: The Influence of Psychological and Environmental Factors Upon the Experience of Pain in Hospital Patients." Chapter 1 in S. Lipton, ed., *Persistent Pain: Modern Methods of Treatment, Vol. 2.* London, Academic Press, 1980

4. A. Levay, et al., "Effects of Physical Illness on Sexual Functioning." Chapter 14 in Leif, *Sexual Problems*

5. Compiled from United States Pharmacopeial Convention, *The Physicians' and Pharmacists' Guide to Your Medicines*. New York, Ballantine Books, 1981. This is suggested as a thorough and easily understood reference to prescription drugs.

6. Suggested by Levay, "Effects," which outlines a more complete method of history-taking.

7. Criteria suggested by J. Lopiccolo, "Treatment of Sexual Concerns by the Primary Care Male Clinician." Chapter 20 in R. Green, ed., *Human Sexuality: A Health Practitioner's Text, 2nd ed.* Baltimore, Williams and Wilkins, 1979

8. M. French, *The Bleeding Heart*. New York, Ballantine Books, 1980, p. 37

9. E. Chigier, "Sexuality of Physically Disabled People." Chapter 7 in M. Elstein, ed., *Clinics in Obstetrics and Gynaecology*. London, W.B. Saunders Co., Ltd., 1980

## BIBLIOGRAPHY

*Aspects of Sexual Medicine: Articles Published in the British Medical Journal.* London; British Medical Association, 1976

Comfort, A. *Sexual Consequences of Disability.* Philadelphia: George F. Stickley Company, 1978

Elstein, M., ed. *Clinics in Obstetrics and Gynaecology,* 1980, 2 London: W.B. Saunders Co., Ltd.

French, M. *The Bleeding Heart.* New York: Ballantine Books, 1980

Green, R., ed. *Human Sexuality: A Health Practitioner's Text, 2nd ed.* Baltimore: Williams and Wilkins, 1979

Hale, G., ed. *The Source Book for the Disabled.* New York: Bantam Books, 1981

Kentsmith, D. and M. Eaton *Treating Sexual Problems in Medical Practice.* New York: Arco Publishing, Inc., 1979

Lief, H., ed. *Sexual Problems in Medical Practice.* Monroe, Wisc., American Medical Association, 1981

Lipton, S., ed. *Persistent Pain: Modern Methods of Treatment, vol. 2.* London: Academic Press, 1980

Munjack, D. and L. Oziel *Sexual Medicine and Counseling in Office Practice.* Boston: Little, Brown and Co., 1980

United States Pharmacopeial Convention *The Physicians' and Pharmacists' Guide to Your Medicines.* New York: Ballantine Books, 1981

Woods, N. *Human Sexuality in Health and Illness.* St. Louis, The C.V. Mosby Co., 1975

# Social Work with Challenged Women: Sexism, Sexuality, and the Female Cancer Experience

Trudy E. Darty, BS
Sandra J. Potter, PhD

**ABSTRACT.** The existence of cancer in a woman usually provokes irrevocable changes in both her body and psyche. When these changes involve an integral part of one's self concept, as in the cases of female breast or reproductive tract cancers, problems of redefinition and transformation of self-image result.

Important issues in the care of female cancer patients cannot be divorced from health care procedures for women in general. This article is an exploration of the daily reality of women who confront the horror and challenge of cancer in areas of their bodies that are intricately related to their sexuality. While attempting to define the problems and discover some feasible social work interventions to alleviate these difficulties, two major issues emerged: the sexual politics of medicine and the psychosocial trauma of cancer. This study will have as its primary focus the second of these two issues.

Historically, cancer has been regarded as synonymous with death. In view of the progress of modern medical science in understanding and treating various types of cancers, this pessimistic prognosis is no longer valid. However, as Kubler-Ross (1969) points out, "Cancer is still for most people a terminal illness" (p. 29). The fact that a patient is told that he or she has cancer brings thoughts of possible death to a conscious awareness. Even if the diagnosis of cancer does not prove to be a fatal one, the existence of the disease usually provokes irrevocable changes in both a patient's

The authors would like to thank Diane Langhorst, MSW, for her comments on an earlier draft of this paper.

body and psyche. When these changes involve an integral part of one's self concept, as in cases of female breast or reproductive tract cancers, problems of redefinition and transformation of self-image result. Important issues in the care of female cancer patients cannot be divorced from health care procedures for women in general. The following is an exploration of the daily reality of women who confront the horror and challenge of cancer in areas of their bodies that are intricately related to their sexuality. While attempting to define the problems and discover some feasible social work interventions to alleviate these difficulties, two major issues emerged: the sexual politics of medicine; and the psychosocial trauma of cancer. This article will have as its primary focus the second of these two issues.

## THE TRAUMA OF CANCER

To understand some of the fundamental problems encountered by female cancer patients when dealing with the medical establishment, one must look at the sexual politics of health care in general (Corea, 1977; Ehrenreich & English, 1979; Ruzek, 1979) and the position and degree of participation of women in the health care industry. The American health care delivery system is dominated by males. The majority of the doctors in the United States are men; and almost all managerial and administrative positions are filled by men (Marieskind, 1980:130-138; Scully, 1980:15).[1]

Male domination of American medicine has resulted in an unequal dichotomy of male doctors and female patients, reflective of traditional sex role patterns in our society, that has instituted a system of paternal social control. The female patient is expected to play the submissive daughter role opposite the all-knowing father figure of the doctor. Her questioning obedience all too often results in medical tragedies, e.g., injury, illness, or death due to unnecessary medical procedures. The condescending attitude of male doctors is common throughout the physician population but is especially pronounced in gynecology (Corea, 1980; Scully, 1980; Wertz & Wertz, 1977). Medical school training and textbooks perpetuate this condescension for future generations of physicians (Campbell, 1973; Ruzek, 1979).

A casual review of medical journals confirms that sexism is alive and well in the medical profession. Both the articles and the advertisements are often offensive. In theory the doctor/patient relationship is one of employee/consumer but in reality more closely resembles parent/child. Prescriptions for librium and valium have replaced the clitorectomy as a way to keep a woman orderly and in her male-defined place. A blatant example of this is one ad for a tranquilizer that reads, "You can't set her free. But you can help her feel less anxious," accompanied by a picture of a housewife imprisoned by housekeeping paraphernalia (Cowan, 1977:36). Most medical journals are filled with such advertisements for mood-altering drugs depicting a neurotic or distressed woman as the likely patient. The success of these ads can be measured by the fact that females are the major consumers of such drugs, constituting two-thirds of the market (Sandelowski, 1981:237-240, Unger, 1979: 403).

It is to this biased medical system that a female cancer patient must entrust herself. A major component of dealing with cancer is that it is an illness so emotionally charged that it affects all dimensions of one's life. A woman must simultaneously deal with: fear of death or disability; disruption of normal daily activity; cancer treatment; assault to sexuality and sexual image; and the resulting victimization and stigmatization.

## Fear of Death or Disability

As previously observed, cancer and death are commonly regarded as synonymous. If diagnosed and treated early, certain types of cancer have a much higher survival rate than other forms of cancer. There has been a 70 percent decrease in death rates from uterine cancer during the last forty years. Current therapy is highly effective when breast cancer is discovered in a localized stage. Recent American Cancer Society (1981) statistics indicate a five-year survival rate of 87 percent (p. 16). However optimistic the prognosis is, the cancer diagnosis still brings the patient face to face with her own mortality. According to Kubler-Ross (1969):

> This . . . can be a blessing or a curse, depending on the manner in which the patient and family are managed in this crucial situation . . . I believe that we should make it a habit to think about death and dying occasionally, I hope before we encounter it in our own life . . . It may be a blessing, therefore, to use the time of illness to think about death and dying in

terms of ourselves, regardless of whether the patient will have to meet death or get an extension of life. (p. 29)

The type of experience described by Kubler-Ross can have an enriching effect upon the quality of life and perception of values. It might prove to be a strengthening experience and afford a real opportunity for personal growth, if utilized in a positive manner. Each woman has to deal with this in her own way. Even if death is not imminent, physical impairment may have to be faced. The more radical mastectomies may leave a woman with impaired use of her affected arm muscles. A hysterectomy obviously renders a woman unable to bear children. Above and beyond the specific mutilations caused by the disease and its treatment are the fears of becoming an invalid, dependent on others for basic needs. Invalidism can be viewed in itself as a form of prolonged death. The word "invalid" used as an adjective reflects this in its definition of being null, void, worthless and valueless.

### Disruption of Normal Daily Activity

Most female cancer patients are forced by the effects of cancer treatment to go through one or more periods of temporary invalidism, during which their normal routine of activity is seriously disrupted. It matters not whether the treatment is surgery, radiation, or chemotherapy. They all contain debilitating side effects. Compelled by physical difficulties to temporarily relinquish many of the relevant roles and activities crucially related to her sense of self, a woman may experience severe emotional stress. She may question both her coping ability and self worth.

Compounding the emotional destructiveness of the disruption of a woman's life is the constant potential for recurrence, a threat that she will have to deal with for as long as she lives. Unlike a simple appendectomy or a broken arm, which will heal and in time be only an unpleasant memory, the cancer patient knows that each episode may be followed by another recurrence of the disease and another round of painful treatment. Having cancer is analogous to a life sentence in prison; there is no permanent escape from its threatening consequences. The medical community's crucial emphasis on the importance of follow-up care because of the potential for recurrence illustrates this fact all too vividly. So uncertainty, with its big "if," becomes a very real factor in all future planning. Human inability to infallibly foretell future events is characteristic of life in general but the threat of disaster and disruption becomes more tangible under these circumstances. Self doubts may arise concerning personal ability to cope if and when the next time arrives. All these extraneous emotions are added to an already overburdened emotional state and need to be realistically examined and resolved.

*Cancer Treatment*

It is unnecessary, within the present context, to discuss the specific details of cancer treatment itself. Suffice it to say that they are often sickening, painful, disfiguring, and unpleasant to undergo. The major side effects of surgery, radiation and chemotherapy are stress producing and have implications for emotional and social adjustment.

However, it is precisely these psychological implications that should be treated with special concern. Physical trauma often seems to induce the greater empathy. Yet psychological stress can be equally as painful as a surgical incision.

Female cancer patients are in the untenable position of being expected to entrust their health and lives to the same medical establishment that for decades has fostered upon women unsafe and inadequately tested cancer-causing drugs and procedures. Women have good reason not to trust the gynecological establishment. As feminist theologian Mary Daly (1978) has so aptly pointed out, "The destruction wrought by gynecology is on display in medical journals" (p. 273-274). It would indeed be foolish to confer implicit trust upon the representatives of a system that is too often implicated as being the perpetrator of the very diseases that women must bring to it for treatment. The vicious cycle of iatrogenic diseases requiring treatments that lead to new health problems, and thus further treatment, illustrates the wide gulf that exists between the idealized Hippocratic concept of healing and the present state of the art (Neuman & Gup, 1981 a,b,c,d).

Armed with her healthy, self-preserving distrust of medicine, a woman must contend with the covert fact that her best interests are not the primary concern of her gynecologist. Sociologists Scully and Bart (1973), in their study of gynecology textbooks published in the United States between 1943 and 1972, suggest that:

examination of gynecology textbooks, one of the primary

professional socialization agents for practitioners in the field, revealed a persistent bias toward greater concern with the patient's husband than the patient herself. Women are consistently described as anatomically destined to reproduce, nurture, and to keep their husbands happy. So gynecology appears to be another of the forces committed to maintaining traditional sex-role stereotypes, in the interest of men and from a male perspective. (p. 273-274)

Daly (1978) speaks of the all encompassing heterosexism imposed by the gynecological culture when she writes:

> The gynecologists are doing "everything possible" to make women "correctly" sexual—that is, Supersexy according to male-identified terms . . . their treatments also are totally controlled by heterosexual suppositions, particularly by the idea that all "normal" women should think/live only in terms of sexual relations with men. (p. 262)

This attitude takes myriad concrete forms. One blatant manifestation is the indiscriminate utilization of vaginal dilators, a routine procedure followed in female pelvic radiation cases to counteract the vaginal atrophying induced by radiation therapy, thus preserving the patient's sexual availability for a male companion. The fact that the use of a dilator during such a physically traumatic period can be painful, degrading, and unnecessary for some women may not be taken into consideration. Instead of the present practice of assuming that all women are identical in their needs and preferences, each woman should be questioned about how important vaginal intercourse is to her personally. There are many women who place little or no importance on this particular expression of sexuality. For such women, another approach to this situation would be to educate the woman and her sexual partner as to alternative methods of sexual satisfaction that do not involve vaginal penetration.

This general disregard for female sensibilities is diffused throughout all forms of female cancer treatment but is probably best illustrated by the dynamics present during pelvic examinations. Emerson (1970) notes that the patient's role requires passivity, self-effacement, and a willingness to relinquish control to the doctor (p. 83). The stylized rituals of gynecological examinations accurately reflect and reinforce the sex-role expectations of the society at large.

## Assault to Sexuality and Sexual Image

Psychosocial issues are of extreme importance when considering the ramifications of female cancers that affect areas of the body intricately related to a woman's sexuality. Women who have such cancers are confronted with a double stigma: the sexuality taboos associated with any serious illness; and the loss of physical attributes culturally defined as fundamental to her femininity. How an individual deals with the latter issues depends, to a great extent, upon her degree of internalization of traditional sex-role socialization.

Within both the general population and the medical profession, there exist many misconceptions and taboos concerning human sexuality, especially among seriously or terminally ill patients. Sexual feelings and desires are often erroneously assumed to be discarded at the hospital entrance or forever abandoned following a diagnosis of serious illness such as cancer. Helping professionals in the medical field are ill-prepared to deal with the vital sexual concerns of clients. There is often an unfounded assumption on the part of medical staff that some other member of the team is discussing sexual questions and concerns. Unfortunately this is an invalid supposition. Doctors and nurses, like many social workers, can be uncomfortable with discussions of sexuality. Compounding this problem is the general ignorance of male doctors concerning female sexuality.

Lois Jaffe (1977), a social worker/patient advocate, and herself a victim of acute leukemia, notes that a self-fulfilling prophecy persists on the part of the patient, spouse and care-giver: a terminally ill individual will neither be interested nor able to function effectively in sex (p. 283). This destructive myth deprives both patients and their partners of a primary source of human solace and emotional validation. Leiber's study (1976) of the communication of affection between cancer patients and their spouses has refuted the contention that serious illness eliminates sexual interests. She recommends that hospital staff recognize the therapeutic value of physical intimacy between couples and facilitate its expression.

An even greater problem for a female cancer patient is the loss or mutilation of physical characteristics directly related to her sexuality; characteristics which our society has decreed intrinsic to her sense of femaleness and self-concept. Surgical procedures utilized in cancer treatment, such as mastectomy, hysterectomy, or vaginectomy, have potent psychosocial and physical consequences. Radiation and chemotherapy can have irreversible side effects (Morra & Potts, 1980; Neuman & Gup, 1981a,b,c,d).[2]

Medical descriptions of the negative consequences of cancer treatment often lack the complete candor that a client needs in order to give informed consent. Women are erroneously led to believe that their sex lives will be unaffected by treatment. For example, while medical practitioners usually assure the prospective patient that a hysterectomy will produce no ill effects on her sexual performance or enjoyment, there are studies that cite post-hysterectomy sexual problems (Newton & Baron, 1976; Woods, 1979). Some women must undergo even more radical cancer surgery on their vaginas and external genitalia. Regardless of claims to the contrary, an artificially reconstructed vagina, designed as a replacement after a vaginectomy, is not as conducive to sexual satisfaction as the woman's original anatomy. The pre-menopausal woman's loss of her ovaries, whether through surgical removal or destructive via radiation or chemotherapy, has a significant impact on her life. She must cope with the physical side effects of an early menopause simultaneously with the emotional aspects of being prematurely forced by circumstances beyond her control into an accelerated aging process while living in a youth-oriented society. A mastectomy is the most visible of the sexually-altering surgeries and requires unique coping skills in our breast-fetishistic culture.

Reaction to any of the previously mentioned psyche-damaging mutilations varies widely among women who must face them. Schain (1976) notes that the concerns displayed and coping mechanisms employed vary with age, marital status, socioeconomic level, and degree of psychological strength (p. 45). Therefore, the psychological and demographic characteristics of this group of women reflects the diversity of the female population at large, since every woman is at risk, regardless of life style or status.

Another factor to be considered is the degree of traditional sex-role socialization. Our society's standards of beauty and femininity are determined by its dominant male faction. Female children are often socialized into believing that male approval is necessary to validate their existence and self-esteem. Thus we note the extreme concern with obtaining and keeping a husband, whose status will be conferred upon his wife. For a woman whose value system follows this norm, mutilation caused by cancer treatment can be psychologically devastating.

For these traditionally-socialized women, the reaction of the male significant other(s) in their support system can be crucial. Schoenberg and Carr (1970) have observed that:

The patient's response to loss of a body part varies with the specific significance of that part to the patient . . . Her reaction to losing a breast will therefore depend to a great extent on her feminine identity, which in turn is determined by her previous relationships with parents, other family members, and more currently, her relationship with her husband. (p. 122-123)

Not all husbands and/or male friends are supportive. Many males seem to utilize avoidance and denial to an extreme degree. Rather than face the reality of the situation, they evade the entire problem by avoiding the patient, either physically, psychologically, or both. When this pattern of male behavior occurs, it can cause emotional anguish for the patient. When a woman is rejected by any family member or friend during a period of such extreme stress and vulnerability, the results are feelings of isolation, pain and alienation. This is particularly true of female cancer patients whose sexual self-image is being challenged and whose self-esteem may be especially fragile.

A concern connected with keeping a male companion is securing one. Consider the woman who is not currently part of a stable heterosexual relationship, but wishes to be. What of her fears, often unfounded, that she will never be able to form such a liaison because of her disfiguring cancer treatment?

For women who have rejected the traditional and stereotypical images of femininity, feelings of personal autonomy and intrinsic self-worth are an invaluable aid in maintaining emotional equilibrium. When a woman's self-esteem is based on her personhood and her own accomplishments, rather than on a transitory beauty that will ultimately fade with age, she is able to face abrupt changes in her body with greater equanimity. Unlike more traditional women, her psychic well-being does not depend on male validation.[3]

### Victimization and Stigmatization

American society can no longer be described as devoutly religious. Power and influence have long since shifted from the religious to the scientific realm. However, some vestiges of religious influence have survived and are insidiously intertwined with scientific pronouncements.

Centuries ago organized religion began teaching that physical suffering was God's punishment for wrong doing and must be endured to atone for sin. The religious doctrine of atonement has been perpetuated by the medical profession. During the 1800s, the scientific explanation of female diseases included the teaching that women's reproductive problems and diseases, including cancer, were the result of bad attitudes and habits (Ehrenreich & English, 1973:30). Witness the scientific community's accusations concerning a woman's personal culpability for certain cancers in her reproductive organs. Cervical cancer is the main target, but breast cancer does not escape sexist comment. In recent years the medical opinion that sexual promiscuity in females contributes to the development of cervical cancer has been widely disseminated (ACS, 1981, p. 16; Epstein, 1979, pp. 486-487, Fox, 1976, p. 19; Labrum, 1976; p. 420; Roddick, 1976, pp. 880-889). Ever since medical researchers have noted that cervical cancers are rare among celibate groups of women, such as nuns, it has been assumed that sexual activity is a component in the development of this disease (Beral, 1974:1037).

Several questionable studies done in the 1950s attempted to link inhibited sexuality and rejection of feminine roles with the pathogenesis of breast cancer (Schain, 1976). As recently as 1978, a doctor associated with cancer research was quoted in a news interview as saying, "Women who lived in conflict with their mothers, who resent sex, who reluctantly accept their roles as females, seem particularly liable to breast cancer" (Shearer, 1978: 16). It appears that women are condemned if they do and condemned if they don't.

The facts do not support such blanket condemnations. A literature review has revealed numerous hypotheses as to the pathogensis of cervical and breast cancers. None has been proven beyond all doubt. Some contributing factors possibly associated with increased risk of cervical cancer are: low socio-economic status; stress; use of synthetic estrogen; a virus; early sexual activity; chronic vaginal and cervical infections; uncircumcised husbands; and sperm, which may in itself be a carcinogen or may act as a vehicle to transfer a cancer virus into cells.[4]

Strong evidence has emerged that socioeconomic class may be a decisive factor. Recent American Cancer Society (1979) statistics indicate that:

> Cervical cancer is more common in low socioeconomic groups. Puerto Rican immigrant women have about four times as much cervical cancer as mainland U.S. women. There is

also more cervical cancer among black women (34 per 100,000) than white women (15 per 100,000). (p. 18)

In view of the fact that the relative economic deprivation experienced by minority communities is well-documented, these data suggest that economic class may be a key variable in identifying high risk populations.

The implication that poor women and/or minority women are any less moral or more sexually active than their more affluent sisters cannot be accepted. To do so would be both elitist and racist. Thus it appears that the lower socioeconomic class lifestyle, with its emotional stresses, poorer quality of diet, housing and medical care, and other environmental factors, seems to be far more directly related to the higher risk of cervical cancer than is any incidence of promiscuity.

Research needs to be interpreted in an objective light. Higgins, Borefreund, Wahrman, and Bendich, Memorial Sloan—Kettering Cancer Center researchers, have noted:

> Seminal components have recently been implicated as contributing factors in the etiology of gynecological malignancies, particularly cancers of the uterine cervix. Although a definite cervical tissue ''oncogen'' remains to be identified, spermatozoa and seminal fluid viruses, acting independently or synergistically as initiators or promotors, are regarded as potential causative agents. (pre-publication draft, p. 8)

If the allegations that sperm may be directly implicated in the pathogenesis of cervical cancer are correct, then it is not promiscuity that we need to be concerned with. Perhaps each adolescent girl's sex education should include: WARNING: SPERM MAY BE HAZARDOUS TO YOUR HEALTH! By ignoring other known or suspected variables and selectively publicizing a female character assassination in the form of a promiscuity charge, our society succeeds once more in blaming the victim.

## PRACTICE IMPLICATIONS

Ideally, social workers should be involved with human issues on two different levels of practice: their personal interaction with individual clients; and the broader perspective of social action as a systems change agent. Each worker cannot be directly involved in every social issue, but an increased measure of awareness within the social work profession regarding the problems endemic to women's health care and support for viable remedies could greatly alleviate client distress by changing the system instead of attributing that distress to individual client pathology. Health care consumers have as much right to dignity, respect and high quality service as do consumers of any other product. When a television or automobile fails to perform adequately, society does not automatically blame the purchaser of the item for its failure. The medical industry should not be exempt from similar responsibility for its vital product, our health care.

On the personal interaction level, one function of social work is to facilitate the essential linkages between clients and existing resource systems. This role is often hampered by the lack of adequate medical social work programs and support services. The scarcity of such services within some inpatient gynecology units appears to be yet another indication of the lower status of women in regards to the priorities of medical funding and allocation of resources.[5] These inequities need to be corrected.

In addition to the utilitarian aspects of social work interventions with female cancer patients, such as arranging for child care or financial aid, direct practitioners need to be prepared to deal with the psychosocial and sexual concerns of their clients. To do so effectively, helping professionals should be aware of and work through their own feelings about death and sexuality, both separately and in combination. It is unrealistic to assume that a health professional can assist a client in working through such emotionally volatile anxieties without personally resolving these issues first.

One way to facilitate this personal awareness for helping professionals is to include courses on sexuality and terminality in their academic curriculums. Writing in the *Journal of Education for Social Work,* Matek (1977) notes:

> A new development in social work education is the offering of human sexuality courses in the graduate curriculum. This focus does not represent a major change in social work practice, but an overdue clarification in an especially difficult area. Because sexual issues are so emotionally charged for most people, it is difficult to learn the required skills necessary for dealing with that aspect of practice without an awareness and working through of some of one's own biases. (p. 50)

Matek observes that the task of eliminating sexual hangups and the restructuring of student attitudes is the most challenging and arduous dimension of such courses. Successful resolution of personal anxieties will enable social workers to be more supportive in these sensitive areas.

Along with the social history, a non-judgemental sexual history should be obtained from the client. The fact that clients do not often bring up sexual concerns does not mean such concerns are non-existent. Social workers may often have to be the ones that initiate discussion of these sensitive topics. When interviewing a client, nothing should be assumed. Social workers should be aware that preconceived notions are especially destructive communication barriers when discussing such an intensely personal facet of life experience. The client is the only person qualified to define herself. Some suggestions for an effective interview could include open-ended questions on the following: fears concerning the effect of cancer treatment on sexual expression; current sexual activity and desired future sexual activity; reaction of sexual partner to the cancer and the cancer therapy; the degree of emotional investment in various body parts, e.g., breasts, uterus; and importance of vaginal intercourse to both the cancer patient and her partner. Through both verbal and non-verbal cues permission should be conveyed to the client to discuss any aspect of her sexuality or sexual concerns. Finally, no presumptions regarding sexual preference (heterosexual, lesbian, bisexual, or celibate) should be made before discussing the issue with the client.

Two common assumptions need to be examined in regards to sexual counseling with female cancer patients. First, most of the literature and self-help groups available to these women make the heterosexist assumption that a major concern is retaining a traditionally-defined cosmetic and sexual attractiveness. For a growing number of women this is of little significance. Many women, regardless of sexual preference, define themselves and their priorities independent of patriarchal criteria. Medical social workers need to be cognizant of this fact in order to maximize their effectiveness with such clients, and ought to be in the vanguard of a movement away from a preoccupation with male interests even when the client is female. Instead, it is crucial that a primary focus on addressing women's self-defined needs and concerns be instituted.

A second assumption is that all significant others within the woman's natural support system will function effectively in her best interest. All practitioners that do psychosocial counseling with female cancer patients/clients must recognize the reality that many males in this system may not be emotionally able to play an adequately supportive role, especially during periods of hospitalization. Sufficient evidence exists of a generalized difference between the coping behaviors and attitudes displayed toward serious illness by females and males respectively to warrant additional research on this question (Davidson & Gordon, 1979:173-179; Nathanson, 1978: 23-32; Stoll, 1978:171-176).

A social worker's most valuable contribution to a client's psychosocial adjustment may be the nurturing of the client's inherent coping skills,[6] thus assisting a woman to utilize her current life crisis as a vehicle for positive growth and strengthening self-awareness. A byproduct of a bout with cancer can be a fertile period of intense, evolutionary self-enhancement. When a woman's power and validity are embedded securely within herself, her life-confronting capabilities are augmented and she is less vulnerable to the constant barrage of sexism. As feminist poet Audre Lorde (1979) has observed, "What is there possibly left for us to be afraid of, after we have dealt face to face with death and not embraced it? Once I accept the existence of dying, as a life process, who can ever have power over me again?" (p. 50).

On the social action level, social workers must be aware of the prevalent sexism in the medical profession, both historically and currently. Exploring the relationship between power and illness, Krause (1977) notes:

Sexism is found in the health care setting in four main ways: as direct behavior of one group towards another; as an institutional pattern of medical treatment behavior; as a form of information control over women relating to their special problems; and as an aspect of the profit-motivated behavior of the medical-industrial complex. (p. 103).

As long as women remain powerless, they will continue to be exploited as consumers because the profits generated by medical care for women are too substantial to be voluntarily relinquished by the health care industry.

One viable approach to confronting this entrenched system is to actively support the Women's Health Movement. This assertive movement has a dual purpose: the wide dissemination of current research and practical medical information to the individual woman;

and the challenging of the present health care system (Cowan, 1977). At this point in time, the indigenous self-help clinics that have mushroomed under the guidance of the Women's Health Movement do not have the sophisticated facilities and technology required to enable them to offer direct care to cancer patients. They are basically limited to providing preventative and routine gynecological and obstetrical care. However, the Women's Health Movement has played a crucial role in facilitating beginning reforms in the patriarchal health care system. Ruzek (1979) notes that, "The women's health movement shows how incremental social change occurs on many levels and how changes in self-conception and self-determination can stimulate widespread social action" (p. 234). Through the demystification of medicine and self-help knowledge of their own bodies, women can regain control over their health and reproductive lives.

Social workers can support and/or do research in the psychosocial variables of female cancer. Many aspects require further development. For instance, currently available prostheses for mastectomy patients often leave a lot to be desired.[7] Terese Lasser, the founder of Reach to Recovery, has an informal theory that there are so few good prostheses for breasts because mastectomies happen to women. If they cut off men's testicles, they would have worked up a great replacement by now (Rollins, 1977:185). Social workers can facilitate new developments through various measures, including documentation of need and agitation for more equitable allocation of resources.

Changes must be facilitated in the hospital environment to encourage ongoing intimacy for patients and their spouse or lover. It is crucial that physical intimacy not be denied during a time when the curative power and comfort of human touch is most needed. In addition, alternative care situations such as the hospice team approach need to be promoted.

Social workers need to examine the physical environment of their offices and agencies to ensure that they are barrier free and provide easy access to the physically challenged. Many cancer patients experience a loss of mobility, either temporarily or permanently, that can erect substantial barriers to the continuation of professional and social life. In recent years, physically challenged activists and their temporarily abled allies have made great progress in securing increased accessibility to public facilities but much remains to be done.

Increased opportunities for women throughout the health care professions need to be promoted. Only when women share more equally in the power inherent at policy-making levels will the medical hierarchy no longer be able to exert such a crushing measure of social control over women as a group. Women who are faced with the difficult battle against cancer have a right to expect that the professionals who offer help during this time of crisis will be allies, not double agents. Anyone who functions as a patient advocate, in whatever capacity, has a responsibility to ensure that all their efforts are truly in the *best* interests of these physically and psychologically challenged women.

## REFERENCE NOTES

1. Gynecologists are often the primary physicians for female patients with reproductive tract cancers. Gynecological demographics are reflective of the overall medical community. According to 1980 American Medical Association statistics, approximately 12 percent of obstetrician-gynecologists practicing in the U.S. are women. There are 467,679 physicians practicing in this country, 44,707 or slightly more than 9.5 percent are women.
2. Two examples of the damage that can be done by radiation are: intestinal damage that may lead to the cancer patient requiring a colostomy; and painful fibrosis which can result from high level radiation or the overlapping of radiation fields. Some chemotherapy drugs have been known to cause kidney damage, diabetes, and a second cancer.
3. Research on self-esteem and self-image of female cancer patients has been seriously lacking. However, since the authors have completed this article, Wendy Schain has published a most valuable article entitled "Self-Esteem, Sexuality, and Cancer Management." Schain's article can be found in *Coping With Medical Issues: Living and Dying With Cancer,* edited by Paul Ahmed (New York: Elsevier North Holland, Inc., 1981) and *Psychotherapeutic Treatment of Cancer Patients,* edited by Jane G. Goldberg, Ph.D. (New York: The Free Press, 1981).
4. See The Boston Women's Health Book Collective, *Our Bodies Ourselves,* 2nd Edition Revised (New York: Simon and Schuster, 1976); *1982 Cancer Facts & Figures;* Beral, pp. 1037-1040; Arthur C. Carr and Bernard Schoenberg, "Object-Loss and Somatic Symptom Formation," in Schoenberg, *Loss and Grief,* pp. 38-41; Cowan, pp. 26-27; Abraham Ravich, *Preventing V.D. and Cancer by Circumcision* (New York: Philosophical Library, 1973); Paul J. Higgins, et al., "Appearance of Foetal Antigens in Somatic Cells After Interaction with Heterologous Sperm," *Nature* Vol. 257 (October 9, 1975), pp. 488-489; and Paul J. Higgins, et al., *"In Vitro* Consequences of Sperm-Somatic Cell Interactions," *European Journal of Cancer* (1980), prepublication draft.
5. Discussions that the authors have had during the past six years with medical social workers and oncology gynecology patients at two major university medical centers and various community hospitals substantiate the observation that inpatient oncology gynecology units are not adequately staffed with social workers. This lack of staffing has resulted in minimal supportive counseling for patients that requested a social worker and none for those that did not. Clearly there is a strong need for more assertive case finding on the part of social workers assigned to oncology gynecology units. Such a need could be easily documented by physicians, nurses, and hospital chaplins. A social work director at one community hospital told the authors that emphasis was placed on discharge planning rather than supportive counseling because hospital administrators saw financial profit in the first but not in the lat-

ter. For a discussion of priorities of medical funding and allocation of resources see "The Valium and Breast Cancer Affair" by D. F. Horrobin, *International Journal of Women's Studies,* Vol. 4, #1, 1981.

6. For a model dealing with the psychosocial rehabilitation of hospitalized oncology patients which was found to be effective in use with gynecologic cancer patients see: Mary Ann Capone, et al., "Crisis Intervention: A Functional Model for Hospitalized Cancer Patients," *American Journal of Orthopsychiatry* Vol. 49, No. 4 (October 1979), pp. 598-607.

7. Not all women may want to utilize a prothesis following mastectomy. Writing of her own experiences with cancer, Lorde declares that, "The emphasis upon wearing a prothesis is a way of avoiding having women come to terms with their own pain and loss, and thereby with their own strength" (Lorde, p. 59). For further discussion of this perspective see: Audre Lorde, The Cancer Journals (Spinisters Ink, RD 1, Argyle, New York 12809), 1981. However, for those women who feel more psychically comfortable with a prosthesis, the best possible should be available.

## REFERENCES

Beral, Valeries. "Cancer of the Cervix: A Sexually Transmitted Infection?" *Lancet,* May 25, 1974, 1037-1040.

1980 Cancer Facts & Figures. New York: American Cancer Society, Inc., 1979.

1982 Cancer Facts & Figures. New York: American Cancer Society, Inc., 1981.

Corea, Gene. "The Caesarean Epidemic." *Mother Jones,* July, 1980, 28-42.

Corea, Gena. *The Hidden Malpractice.* New York: William Morrow & Co., 1977.

Campbell, Margaret. *"Why Would a Girl Go Into Medicine?" Medical Education in the United States: A Guide for Women.* Old Westbury, New York: The Feminist Press, 1973.

Cowan, Belita. *Women's Health Care: Resources, Writings, Bibliographies.* Ann Arbor, Michigan: Anshen Publishing, 1977.

Daly, Mary. *Gyn/Ecology: The Metaethics of Radical Feminism.* Boston: Beacon Press, 1978.

Davidson, Laurie & Laura Kramer Gordon. *The Sociology of Gender.* Chicago: Rand McNally, 1979.

Ehrenreich, Barbara & English, Deirdre. *Complaints and Disorders: The Sexual Politics of Sickness.* Old Westbury, New York: The Feminist Press, 1973.

Ehrenreich, Barbara & English, Deirdre. *For Her Own Good: 150 Years of the Experts' Advice to Women.* Garden City, New York: Anchor Books, 1979.

Emerson, Joan P. "Behavior in Private Places: Sustaining Definitions of Reality in Gynecological Examinations" in *Recent Sociology,* No. 2, edited by H. P. Dreitzel. New York: Macmillan Co., 1970, 74-97.

Epstein, Samuel S. *The Politics of Cancer.* Garden City, New York: Anchor Press/Doubleday, 1979.

Fox, Bernard H. "The Psychosocial Epidemiology of Cancer" in *Cancer: The Behavioral Dimensions,* edited by J. W. Cullen, B. H. Fox, and R. N. Isom. New York: Raven Press, 1976, 11-22.

Horrobin, D. F. "The Valium and Breast Cancer Affair: Lessons Relating to the Involvement of Women in Health Care Research and Policy," *International Journal of Women's Studies,* Vol. 4, #1, 1981, 19-26.

Higgins, Paul G. et al. "In Vitro Consequences of Sperm-Somatic Cell Interactions." *European Journal of Cancer,* 1980 prepublication draft.

Jaffe, Lois. "The Terminally Ill" in *The Sexually Oppressed,* edited by Harvey L. & Jean S. Gochros. New York: Association Press, 1977, 277-292.

Krause, Elliott A. *Power & Illness: The Political Sociology of Health and Medical Care.* New York: Elsevier, 1977.

Kubler-Ross, Elisabeth. *In Death and Dying.* New York: Macmillan Publishing Co., Inc., 1969.

Labrum, Anthony H. "Psychological Factors in the Etiology and Treatment of Cancer of the Cervix." *Clinical Obstetrics and Gynecology,* Vol. 19, #2, June, 1976, 419-430.

Leiber, Lillian, et al. "The Communication of Affections Between Cancer Patients and Their Spouses." *Psychomatic Medicine,* Vol. 38, #6, November/December 1976, 379-389.

Lorde, Audre. "Breast Cancer: A Black Lesbian Feminist Experience." *Sinister Wisdom,* 10, Summer 1979, 44-61.

Lorde, Audre. *The Cancer Journals.* Argyle, New York: Spinisters Ink, 1981.

Marieskind, Helen I. *Women in the Health System: Patients, Providers, and Programs.* St. Louis: C. V. Mosby Co., 1980.

Matek, Ord. "A Methodology for Teaching Human Sexuality to Social Work Students." *Journal of Education for Social Work,* Vol. 13, #3, Fall 1977, 50-55.

Morra, Marion & Eve Potts. *Choices: Realistic Alternatives In Cancer Treatment.* New York, New York: Avon Books, 1980.

Nathanson, Constance A. "Illness and the Feminine Role: A Theoretical Review" in *Dominant Issues in Medical Sociology,* edited by Howard D. Schwartz & Cary S. Kart. Reading, MA: Addison-Wesley Publishing Co., 1978, 23-31.

Neuman, Jonathan & Gup, Ted. "The War on Cancer: First Do No Harm." *Washington Post,* October 18, 1981, A1 & A14-A15. (a)

Neuman, Jonathan & Gup, Ted. "The War on Cancer: First Do No Harm." *Washington Post,* October 19, 1981, A1 & A26-A27. (b)

Neuman, Jonathan & Gup, Ted. "The War on Cancer: Anatomy of a Clinic." *Washington Post,* October 20, 1981, A1 & A18-A19. (c)

Neuman, Jonathan & Gup, Ted. "The War on Cancer: Anatomy of a Drug." *Washington Post,* October 21, 1981, A1 & A10-A11. (d)

Newton, Niles & Baron, Enid. "Reactions to Hysterectomy: Fact or Fiction." *Primary Care,* Vol. 3. #4, December 1976, 781-801.

Roddick, J. W. "Gynecologic Disease in Young, Sexually Active Women." *American Journal of Obstetrics and Gynecology,* Vol. 126, #7, December 1, 1976, 880-889.

Rollin, Betty. *First You Cry.* New York: New American Library, Inc., 1977.

Ruzek, Sheryl Burt. *The Women's Health Movement: Feminist Alternatives to Medical Control.* New York: Praeger Publishers, 1979.

Sandelowski, Margarete. *Women, Health, and Choice.* Englewood Cliffs, New Jersey: Prentice-Hall, Inc., 1981.

Schain, Wendy S. "Psychological Issues in Counseling Mastectomy Patients." *The Counseling Psychologist,* Vol. 6, #2, 1976, 45-49.

# Women's Health/Sexuality: The Case of Menopause

## Constance Lindemann, Dr PH

There are many areas where women's health interfaces with women's sexuality. Menopause is such an area. Menopause is a life cycle event that marks entry into the non-reproductive years. It is a universal experience for women and on the average women live for more than 25 years beyond menopause. These years have been largely discounted and menopausal and postmenopausal women have been denigrated in popular and medical views and in the physiological and psychosocial treatment of menopausal symptoms. This chapter will examine issues in menopause from the social work value perspective of self-determination. Traditional and alternative attitudes and treatment of menopause will be discussed as well as the implications for social work education and practice.

The purpose of this article is to explore menopause as a specific example of women's health related to women's sexuality in order to understand how women have been denigrated and deprived of self-determination and to provide a basis for the promotion of self-determination for women by social workers. It is relevant to social workers in health care settings, women's resource centers, and all other social work settings where women are clients and patients.

## SELF-DETERMINATION

Self-determination, the ability to make decisions and participate in the helping process, is a firmly established value in social work and recognized as an important part of the process. It is less well recognized in the health care model. However, in order to maintain and restore health it is a necessary part of that process as well. This is evident from the experience of women in childbirth. A good childbirth experience appears to be related more to how fully a woman participates in the experience and to how women make their own decisions than to how easy the birth is, how long or short the labor is, or even where the birth takes place (Rogers, 1979). The health care model should provide for the systematic cultivation and use of self-determination. Too often it systematically deprives the patient of self-determination. Women, in health care as in other spheres of life, have been deprived of self-determination. The mildest form of deprivation in the medical situation is when the physician walks into the examining room and says, "Hello, *Jean,* I'm *Dr. Smith.*" This occurs regardless of the age of the patient and immediately establishes the physician as superior in the power relationship. At the other extreme is the ultimate deprivation of self-determination, the administration or prescription of drugs; particularly, in the case of women, tranquilizers. Drugs are for the "complaining woman," the woman who is perhaps trying to express what is standing in the way of self-determination. At the very point when she needs self-determination to effect a real cure, to do something about her life and her environment, she is deprived by a drug prescription. Drugged people don't do or say anything. That's one of the purposes of drugs. Drugged or tranquilized women are docile (good) patients and docile (good) members of society. A little addicted, maybe, but "good." And then the addiction becomes *her problem*. This is a common occurrence. Iatrogenic addiction, addiction which is caused by medically prescribed drugs, is a major health problem among women (Halas, 1979; Damman & Soler, 1979; Wolcott, 1979).

The widespread administration and prescription of drugs is not just the excessive use or misuse of an otherwise valuable medical resource; it is the logical outcome of a health care model that does not recognize and systematically cultivate self-determination as an essential component of health. It is a basic contradiction in health care that the patient must give up self-determination, an essential component of health, in order to acquire the professional skills and knowledge that may be necessary for the maintenance and restoration of health. It has long been assumed that relinquishing self-determination, "placing yourself in the hands of the physician," is a necessary condition for maintaining and restoring one's health. This is not only unnecessary; it is, in fact, detrimental. Maintaining and restoring health requires the full power of the patient in an egalitarian, cooperative effort with the professional who provides the necessary special skills and training. An example and model for this approach has been provided by Norman Cousins in his book, *The Anatomy of an Illness* (1979). The currently prevailing health care model must be changed from one in which the patient is deprived of power to one in which the power of the patient is systematically cultivated and where he/she has a say in what's happening, what needs to be done, and what will be done, with the professional providing the necessary skills and knowledge to aid the patient. In recent years the health consumer movement—and especially the Women's Health Movement—has been effecting this social change (Boston Women's Health Collective, 1976).

Women have been especially deprived of self-determination in those areas where health is related to women's sexuality. The unique reproductive capacity and sexual characteristics of women, which should be a source of pride and power and the basis for self-determination, are those very areas where women have been manipulated and oppressed. As Bart and Perlmutter put it: "those very things that make women different from men have too long been defined as deviant, diseased or undesirable" (1981).

## PERSPECTIVES ON MENOPAUSE

### Popular and Medical Views

Menopause is perhaps the primary area of health related sexuality where women have been defined as deviant, diseased and undesirable. In the popular stereotype of the menopausal woman she is exhausted, irritable, unsexy, hard to live with, irrationally depressed, and unwillingly suffering a "change" that marks the end of her active (re) productive life (Boston Women's Health Collective, 1976). The medical view, equally negative, is probably more influential due to the weight of professional expertise. At a conference on menopause and aging sponsored by the U.S. Department of Health, Education and Welfare in 1971, at which there was not a single woman participant, a Johns Hopkins gynecologist characterized menopausal women as "a caricature of their younger selves at their emotional worst" (Bart & Perlmutter, 1981). In 1973 the past president of the American Geriatric Society described menopause as a chronic and incapacitating deficiency disease that leaves women with flabby breasts, wrinkled skin, fragile bones, and loss of ability to have or enjoy sex (Sloan, 1980).

These myths are perpetrated by the medical profession based on clinical experience and, perhaps, by personal bias and lack of objectivity. Recent research has shown that only 25% of women see their physicians for menopausal symptoms. Therefore clinical papers do not reflect the experiences of the majority of women (Bart and Perlmutter, 1981). A 1933 study, one of the few studies available on the incidence of menopausal symptoms, indicated that of 1000 women studied 15-20% had no clinical symptoms at all (Sloan, 1980). Another study showed that perhaps 5-10% of 100 women had persistent and severe symptoms (Dewhurst, 1976). It may be concluded, then, that the remaining 70-80% may have some symptoms, but that these are mild enough to be ignored.

## The Views of Women and Women's Scholarship

Women's studies scholarship in health and health related areas indicates that menopausal women, themselves, do not view menopause as the severe and incapacitating condition that popular and medical views portray. Neugarten (1963) found that menopause was not a particularly important experience for the women in her study. Only one out of four thought menopause was a major source of worry. Negative views of women's sexuality have also been contradicted by Neugarten's research. Sixty-five percent of the women in the study said there was no effect on their sexuality, and of the remainder, 45% found sexual activity became less important and half thought sexual relations were more enjoyable because menstruation and fear of pregnancy were removed (Boston Women's Health Collective, 1976).

Bart and Perlmutter (1981) cite research that shows the influence of social and cultural factors on menopause. The transition to nonreproductive years was harder for women who were giving up highly valued roles; those who were very invested in their role as mother were more anxious going through the menopause than they were after it; and women who were low in self esteem and life satisfaction were most likely to have difficulty during menopause. Cross cultural studies suggest that depression in menopause is not as much related to physiological changes as to social and cultural factors. Depression is related to role loss or the prospect of loss of roles such as the wife or mother roles. Lack of self esteem rather than any hormonal changes seemed to account for the incidence of menopausal depression. They conclude that greater stress due to social and cultural factors maximizes the distress and symptoms of menopause and, conversely, less stress due to social and cultural factors minimizes menopausal distress and symptoms.

## TREATMENT OF MENOPAUSE

### Estrogen Replacement Therapy

These divergent attitudes toward menopause are matched by divergent diagnoses and divergent treatments. One point of view regards menopause as a diseased state caused by estrogen deficiency requiring long term use of estrogen replacement therapy (ERT). The leading proponent of ERT is Dr. Robert Wilson, who has been criticized by the medical profession and the United States Food and Drug Administration. The Wilson Research Foundation was funded by drug companies that obviously have a vested interest in the sale of the drugs (Bart and Perlmutter, 1981). It is Wilson's belief that estrogen can cure twenty-six symptoms supposedly caused by menopause and that women should take estrogen for the rest of their lives in order to remain *Feminine Forever* which is the title of his book (Wilson, 1966). The book was excerpted in many women's magazines and has influenced, or perhaps more accurately frightened, women into ERT.

The more conservative medical view is that menopause is an expectable, if troublesome, phase in a women's life and that ERT is justified for only two symptoms of menopause, vaginal atrophy (dryness and thinning of the vaginal walls) and hot flashes (Utian, 1976). Its effectiveness for a third, osteoporosis (thinning of the bones)—often the cause of bone fractures in older women—is still a matter of debate. The more conservative view also takes into account the risks of ERT: Women who received ERT were 4.5 to 8 times more likely to develop uterine cancer than were women who did not receive ERT. Other possible risks and side effects of ERT include nausea, breast tenderness or swelling, alteration of the uterine lining, liver problems including increased risk of liver tumors, swelling or retention of fluid which aggravates other physical problems, skin rash, hair loss, and inability to use contact lenses (Stewart et al., 1979). This more conservative view of ERT advocates the use of ERT for only those cases where symptoms are severe and incapacitating (Sloan, 1980) and the use of locally applied estrogen preparations for vaginal atrophy that do not increase the risk of cancer (Dewhurst, 1976).

Between these two extreme views of ERT—universal, routine, long term use and cautious, limited use—are all shades of opinion and, consequently, great variation in the use of ERT among physicians. The United States Food and Drug Administration, in its 1976 advisory bulletin to U.S. physicians, advocated the conservative approach (Stewart et al., 1979). The necessity of self-determination is clearly indicated. "The use of estrogen in the climacteric should not be left to the physician alone; all women should be informed of the risks and given the choice to decide whether the benefits are worth the risks" (Sloan, 1980); and, "the decision the woman makes to initiate ERT must be an informed one. The risks and benefits of ERT should be fully explored and alternatives such as nutritional supplementation and exercise programs presented" (Frigate-Woods, 1981).

## Alternative Physiological Treatment

An alternative physiological approach to menopausal symptoms is based on diet, exercise, nutritional supplements, and vaginal lubrication for those symptoms that are attributed to menopause: osteoporosis, hot flashes, and vaginal atrophy.

Exercise and diet have been demonstrated to have an effect on bone loss (osteoporosis). Bone density depends on the extent to which bones are used. The incidence of osteoporosis is lower in populations where individuals are physically active (Seaman and Seaman, 1978); therefore a regular exercise program is recommended for the prevention of osteoporosis. In addition to exercise it has been shown that diet effects bone loss. Vegetarians have lower rates of bone loss than omnivores (Wachman and Bernstein, 1968; Ellis et al., 1972). Nutritional supplements such as vitamins and calcium also help to prevent bone loss (Seaman and Seaman, 1978).

Hot flashes are alleviated by an herbal remedy, ginseng, and vitamin supplements. Ginseng research is carried on extensively outside of the United States, particularly in Russia and Japan and has been shown to have considerable effects on the thermo-vascular system and on the biochemistry of the body. Although there have been no studies specific to the effects of ginseng on hot flashes, it is recommended on the basis of these thermo-vascular studies, and on the basis of practical experience of women and physicians with the herb. Vitamin supplements, particularly vitamin E, have also been shown to alleviate hot flashes (Seaman & Seaman, 1978). The main problem in vaginal atrophy is that the vagina does not get sufficient lubrication. There is no doubt that ERT remedies this problem, but there are alternative remedies. One remedy is regular orgasm. The vagina responds to sexual activity by lubricating and the increased blood supply to the vagina during orgasm maintains the health and lubricating ability of the vagina. This may be accomplished by sexual activity with a partner—either male or female—or by masturbation. In the case of sex with a partner, particularly male, where penile penetration of the vagina takes place, a longer period of love-making before penetration may be required as the vaginal lubrication of older women takes more time than in younger women. Local lubricants such as KY jelly or other harmless lubricants may be used to relieve the symptoms of a dry vagina and/or to enhance sexual intercourse. Locally applied preparations of estrogen cream may also be used. These are assumed to be safer than ERT, however there are no data on the affects of absorbing these preparations into the system from the vagina (Seaman and Seaman, 1978).

The leading proponent of these alternative treatments is Barbara Seaman, a women's health activist and science writer who, with her husband Gideon Seaman, a psycho-pharmacologist, wrote the book *Women and the Crisis in Sex Hormones* (1978) which provides a review of research in diet, exercise and nutritional supplements in the treatment of menopausal symptoms and some practical guidelines for women who wish to explore these alternatives.

### Traditional Psycho-social Treatment

The widespread use of prescription drugs by women and the problems that result have been discussed in the introduction to this paper. Tranquilizers are often given for symptoms attributed to menopause (Boston Women's Health Collective, 1976; Reitz, 1977; Weideger, 1977; Cooper 1976). They are ineffective in the treatment of menopausal symptoms (Notman and Nadelson, 1978; Stewart et al., 1979). They are promoted for that purpose by the drug companies with advertising directed to physicians that show emotionally distraught and complaining women (Weideger, 1977) and go so far as to suggest them for the symptoms that bother *him* the most (Boston Women's Health Collective, 1976; Bart and Perlmutter, 1981).

Traditional psychoanalysis shares the same negative views of menopause and menopausal women as the medical profession. In Deutsch's view (Bart & Perlmutter, 1981) the menopausal woman "reached her natural end—her partial death—as servant of the species"; menopause was a blow to her vanity because "with the lapse of the reproductive service, her beauty vanishes and usually the warm, vital flow of feminine emotional life as well." Deutsch's conclusion that "feminine, loving women would fare best at menopause" is contradicted by the sociological and cultural evidence discussed in the section on women's studies scholarship. Traditional psychotherapy, then, not only did not help, but actually exacerbated the problem by advocating the very roles that have been shown to be dysfunctional at menopause and then blaming the victim for not accepting these roles.

The early views expressed by Deutsch are evident in more recent theory and practice. The American Psychological Association 1975 Task Force on Sex Bias and Sex Role Stereotyping in Psychotherapeutic Practice found sexist use of psychoanalytic concepts, fostering of traditional sex roles, bias in expectations for and devaluation of women, and response to women as sex objects (Sturdivant, 1980).

### Alternative Psycho-social Treatment

The alternative treatment that has been largely initiated and developed by women health activists, both professional and non-professional, is to develop feminist therapy and to provide information and consciousness raising in groups and seminars. Feminist therapy rejects the social adjustment model in favor of change in the direction of increased autonomy and self-determination and focuses on the cultural and social oppression of women (Sturdivant, 1980). Consciousness raising groups provide the opportunity for women to share their experience and realize that what women thought were individual problems are in fact common problems that have a social cause and probably a political solution (Sturdivant, 1980). Therefore, in addition to individual change, social consciousness and action is a goal for both therapists and clients. As a result of this process of connecting sociocultural attitudes and personal feelings, one menopausal woman was surprised to find that her hot flashes, once considered uncomfortable, had become pleasurable (Weidegger, 1977). In this case, as in many others, menopause and menopausal symptoms were redefined by women and the socially prevalent negative definitions were rejected.

## IMPLICATIONS FOR SOCIAL WORK

Traditional treatments models for women have been questioned and shown to be ineffective at best and harmful at worst. Social work needs to develop and expand alternative treatment models (Gottlieb, 1980). The feminist orientation has been shown to be consistent with the social work orientation (Berlin and Kravetz, 1981), and consciousness raising as a skill and tool in social work has been demonstrated (Longres and McCleod, 1980). In fact, rather than alternative models, these models which are more consistent with the social work orientation of person-in-situation, should be included as basic models in social work education and practice. Consciousness raising should be taught in schools of social work as a basic approach to helping people and used regularly in practice. An example of the social work use of consciousness raising is the CR group for obese women (Flack & Grayer, 1975). In addition, new and diverse conceptual models consistent with the values and orientation of social work and reflecting the experience of women should be developed and expanded (Lindemann, 1982a, 1982b).

Resource development and program planning is another area that is needed. Helping people obtain resources includes developing new programs as well as utilizing, expanding, and supporting programs already in existence and helping women develop their own resources. Alternative programs may be developed within traditional agencies or as free standing alternative resources such as Women's Resource Centers and Women's Health Clinics. Programs offered through these agencies include Displaced Homemaker programs and Day Care programs that provide women with opportunities for alternative roles and gynecological health services that are sensitive to the issues of women's health that have been raised in this article. Workers in all settings need knowledge of already existing resources in the community to which they can refer clients. New locales need also to be explored. Mancuso (1980) suggests church, storefront operations, and other "visible, informal, warm, low key'' locales. Workplaces are also an avenue for exploration. Perhaps most important of all is helping women to develop their own resources. Mancuso (1980) cites the Congress of Neighborhood Women in Brooklyn that began with a small education action effort and grew to a well developed organization staffed with women who were trained to work on basic health, education, and welfare issues. The discussion above indicates that health care organizations and social agencies often disregard the needs of women. Social workers in health care setting and in other agencies may be in a position to make organizations more responsive to women. In addition to menopausal problems are examples from childbirth. Many women wish an alternative to the traditional model of birthing where women are drugged and not allowed to participate in the birth of their own babies, let alone including the father of the child in the birthing process. Breast surgery is another example. Physicians and hospitals should be responsive to a woman's need to decide the treatment approach to be used in breast malignancy. Women activists have struggled to change this condition from outside the institutions and organizations. Social workers can lend support by supporting these efforts and by working for change within organizations. Social workers may also act as advocates for women in institutional settings. This role may be fulfilled either by support for the woman in her interaction or by interacting directly with the medical professional on behalf of the woman.

Many social workers are already involved in assertiveness training for women as a way of facilitating the interaction between women and others in their environment. Assertiveness training is designed to enable women to get the information they need and express their own needs. It is a basic tool in self-determination. In the area of women's health/sexuality specific application of this approach is in the interaction between women and medical professionals. Social workers may accomplish this with individuals or with groups. For example, this writer was asked to address a La Leche group (women interested in breast feeding their babies) on how to interact with rural and small town physicians who were not in favor of breast feeding and where the shortage of physicians did not permit shopping around for one who was in sympathy with the woman's choice.

Facilitating interaction may also be accomplished by social work advocacy. Many times a woman needs a supportive person to accompany her in interaction with others, particularly those in a power position.

The discussion on menopause illustrates the role of government in women's health/sexuality. The Food and Drug Administration plays an important role in regulating prescription drugs. Equally important are other branches of the government as the current struggles around abortion illustrate. Social work has regarded, and continues to regard, social action as a significant professional role and is active on the national and local levels on behalf of women. Issues in women's health should be given close scrutiny and supported by social workers and professional social work organizations on every level.

## CONCLUSION

Attitudes toward menopause and the physiological and psycho-social treatment of menopause have been examined from the point of view of self-determination. The purpose was change in attitude and treatment from derogatory attitudes and treatments that may be harmful to women to positive attitudes and treatments in which women are part of the decision making process. The role of social work in direct service, planning, and policy has been indicated. The goal is that every woman should be able to say as Lena Horne has said, "These last 10 or 15 years have been the best of her life. She came to them after a 'marvelous menopause' " (Gavzer 1982, p 19).

## REFERENCES

Bart, Pauline and Perlmutter, Ellen. "The Menopause in Changing Times." in Justice, Betty and Pore, Renata (eds.) *The Second Decade: The Impact of the Women's Movement on American Institutions.* Westport: Greenwood Press, 1981.

Berlin, Sharon and Kravetz, Diane "Women as Victims: A Feminist Social Work Perspective." *Social Work.* 26: 447-449, 1981.

Boston Women's Health Collective. *Our Bodies, Ourselves.* New York: Simon and Schuster, 1976.

Cooper, Wendy. "The Influence of the Media on Women's Requirements for Hormonal Replacement Therapy." in Beard, R.J. (ed.) *The Menopause: Guide to Research and Practice.* Baltimore: University Park Press, 1976.

Cousins, Norman. *The Anatomy of an Illness.* New York: Norton, 1979.

Damman, Grace and Soler, Esta. "Prescription Drug Abuse: A San Francisco Study." *Frontiers,* IV:5-10, 1979.

Dewhurst, C.J., "The Role of Estrogen in Preventative Medicine." in Beard, R.J. (ed.) *The Menopause: A Guide to Current Research and Practice.* Baltimore: University Park Press, 1976.

Ellis, Frey R., Holesh, Schura, and Ellis, John W., "Incidence of Osteoporosis in Vegetarians and Omnivores." *American Journal of Clinical Nutrition.* 25: 555-558, 1972.

Flack, Ruth and Grayer, Elinor D. "A Consciousness Raising Group for Obese Women." *Social Work.* 20: 484-487, 1975.

Frigate-Woods, Nancy. *Health Care of Women: A Nursing Perspective.* St. Louis: C.V. Mosby, 1981.

Gavzer, Bernard. "The Lady is a Champ." *Parade.* February 7, 1982.

Gottlieb, Naomi. *Alternative Services for Women.* New York: Columbia University Press, 1980.

Halas, Mary A. "Sexism in Women's Medical Care." *Frontiers,* IV:11-15, 1979.

Lindemann, Constance. "Sexual Freedom: The Right to Say No." In Review, 1982a.

_____. "Women's Sexuality and Mental Health." *Women and Mental Health.* Women's Studies Program, University of Oklahoma and Oklahoma Humanities Commission. In Press, 1982b.

Longres, John and McLeod, Eileen. "Consciousness Raising and Social Work Practice." *Social Casework.* 61:267-276, 1980.

Mancuso, Arlene. "No Drums, No Trumpets: Working-Class Women." in Norman, Elaine and Mancuso, Arlene (eds) *Women's Issues and Social Work Practice.* Itasca: F.E. Peacock Publishers, Inc., 1980.

Neugarten, Bernice et al. "Women's Attitudes Toward the Menopause." *Vita Humana.* 6: 140-51, 1963.

Perlmutter, Johanna F. "A Gynecological Approach to Menopause." in Notman, Malkah and Nadelson, Carol C. (eds) *The Women Patient: Medical and Psychological Interfaces.* Volume I. New York: Plenum Press 1978.

Reitz, Rosetta. *Menopause: A Positive Approach.* New York: Penguin Books, 1977.

Rogers, Cathy. A film review of "Five Women Five Births: A Film About Choices." *Women & Health,* 4:196-198, 1979.

Seaman, Barbara and Seaman, Gideon. *Women and the Crisis in Sex Hormones.* New York: Bantam Books 1978.

Sloan, Ethel. *Biology of Women.* New York: John Wiley and Sons, 1980.

Stewart, Felicia Hance et al. *My Body, My Health: the Concerned Woman's Guide to Gynecology.* New York: John Wiley and Sons, 1979.

Sturdivant, Susan. *Therapy with Women: A Feminist Philosophy of Treatment.* New York: Springer Publishing Co. 1980.

Utian, W.H. "Scientific Basis for Post-Menopausal Estrogen Therapy: The Management of Specific Symptoms and Rationale for Long-Term Replacement." in Beard, R.J. (ed.) *The Menopause: a Guide to Current Research and Practice.* Baltimore: University Park Press, 1976.

Wachman, Amnon and Bernstein, D.S., "Diet and Osteoporosis," *The Lancet.* 1: 958-959, 1968.

Weidegger, Paula. *Menstruation and Menopause.* New York: Delta Books, 1977.

Wilson, Robert. *Feminine Forever.* New York: M. Evans, 1966.

Wolcott, Ilene. "Women and Psychoactive Drug Use." *Women & Health,* 4:199-201, 1979.

# Treatment Approaches to Sexual Problems with Dual Diagnosis Clients

Thomas R. Jones, LCSW

**ABSTRACT.** A dual diagnosis client is a person with both a mental disorder and a developmental disability. Treatment of sexual problems in dual diagnosis clients has involved behavioral programming, counseling, social skills training and sex education. Case examples are presented to illustrate the application of these treatment modalities. Further research is advocated since the problems of dual diagnosis clients have not been sufficiently addressed. Clinicians must also be aware of oppressive social and institutional factors since they often impinge upon the clinical picture.

"Being mentally retarded is bad enough; being mentally ill, too, makes it many times worse" (Perske, Note 1). Such was the pronouncement by the President's Committee on Mental Retardation in 1979. Since then, this double disability has come to be called *dual diagnosis* or *MD/DD*. Dual diagnosis refers to AAMD, DSM-111, or ICD-9 diagnoses of both a developmental disability and a mental (psychiatric) disorder. These are developmentally disabled persons who have a mental disorder and not persons who have low IQs as a result of a chronic mental disorder. "MD" refers to *mentally disordered* ("mentally ill") whereas "DD" refers to *developmentally disabled* (mental retardation, cerebral palsy, epilepsy, autism or other handicap similar to mental retardation which is not solely physical in nature). As might be expected, such individuals often suffer from the misconceptions and prejudices associated with being both "crazy" and "retarded." When one examines the area of sexuality with regard to such a dual disability, it is not surprising to find that the issues and problems are often quite complex.

## SCOPE OF THE PROBLEM

How prevalent is the problem? Mental retardation is said to occur in 1 out of 10 American families or in about 3% of the population.

This means that there are approximately six million mentally retarded individuals in the United States. Only mental illness, cardiac disease, arthritis, and cancer are more prevalent (Mandelbaum, 1977). Severe psychiatric problems occur much more frequently in mentally retarded persons than in the rest of the population (Committee on Mental Retardation, 1979). Most studies seem to indicate that approximately one-third of the mentally retarded will suffer from some form of diagnosable mental disorder (Menolascino, 1965, 1966, 1970; Philips, 1967; Philps & Williams, 1975; Webster, 1963). If indeed one-third of the mentally retarded do suffer from mental disorders, this would indicate that there are approximately two million dual diagnosis persons in the United States.

Until recently there were almost no resources designed specifically for dual diagnosis persons (Hersh & Brown, 1977; Sarino, 1973; Walker, 1980). These clients were often shuffled between agencies or serviced by facilities that were designed to treat either the mentally disabled *or* the developmetally disabled. Employees in psychiatric clinics and hospitals frequently knew very little about developmental disabilities, habilitation programs, or the needs of developmentally disabled clients. In psychiatric hospitals dual diagnosis clients were often labeled as "retarded" by other residents and were sometimes teased, abused, or scapegoated. On the other hand, those who worked with agencies for the developmentally disabled often had very little mental health training. If a client was served by such a facility, various mental disorders often went unrecognized or untreated. In addition to the lack of agency resources, many psychiatrists, social workers, and other mental health professionals often ignored the area of mental retardation (Gualtieri, 1979; Hayes, 1977; Heaton-Ward, 1977; Potter, 1965; Scanlon, 1978; Selan, 1976; Winokur, 1974). In an attempt to address some of these issues, a specialized, dual diagnosis, inpatient unit (ward) was developed at one of the state hospitals. This article is concerned with the treatment of sexual problems with persons who have resided on that unit, persons with dual diagnoses.

## REVIEW OF THE LITERATURE

There appears to be no published literature regarding the sexual problems of dual diagnosis persons. There are, however, numerous articles regarding the sexual problems of the developmentally disabled. Likewise, there are a fair number of articles regarding the sexual problems of mentally disordered persons and the relationships between mental disorders and sexuality. In a review of the literature in 1978, one author found over 70 articles regarding sexuality and psychiatric disorders and over 110 articles regarding sexuality and mental retardation (Sha'Ked, 1978). Since dual diagnosis persons have both disabilities, one may cautiously draw some inferences from studies of both populations.

The interrelationship between mental disorders and sexuality has long been a concern to professionals. As early as 1838, Esquiral published a textbook in psychiatry that included "passionate" causes of mental illness (Winokur, 1969). But most of the literature to date is either theoretical or is based solely on clinical observations. The need for hard data has been a concern to many (Pinderhughes, Grace, & Reyna, 1972). There is some research evidence to indicate a positive correlation between depression and a loss of sexual interest (Beck, 1968). There are also numerous reports of sexual preoccupation during the manic episodes of bipolar disorders (Andreason, 1981; Gerner, 1981; Small & Small, 1976; Tsuang, 1975). In a review of research on the subject back in 1969, Winokur concluded that manic-depressive illness and chronic brain syndrome appeared to affect sexual life, but that there was no evidence of this in neurosis, schizophrenia, or any other mental disorder. More recently, Marks (1976) mentions depression and social anxiety as two possible contributing factors to sexual problems but points out that there is simply little conclusive research in the area.

The literature regarding developmental disabilities is no more enlightening. Most authors agree that mild levels of mental retardation do not have a significant influence on sexual desire, but little data are available. Sexual exploitation by others is often reported (Small & Small, 1976). But, again, there is no substantiating research in the area. Likewise, there are no data to support the idea of a high frequency of sex offenses (Hall, 1974). One would imagine that lack of physical activity, impoverished social experience, neurological and endocrinal factors, widespread use of medication, and frequent medical problems could all be influencing factors on the sexual behavior of the mentally retarded. One must conclude, however, that there is simply no conclusive research in the area.

Regarding the relationship of mental disorders or developmental disabilities to sexuality, one can only hope that the plethora of theories, opinions, and observations in this area will eventually lead to more research. Although this article itself is based on clinical observations rather than empirical research, it is written to help fill a gap in an area where there has been no previous literature and will, hopefully, be of some heuristic value. With this understood, this article will proceed with describing the four approaches that are utilized in treating the sexual problems and concerns of dual diagnosis clients. These include the two individual approaches of *behavioral programming* and *counseling* plus the two group approaches of *social skills training* and *sex education*. Each of these treatment approaches will be discussed in turn, using case examples.

## TREATMENT APPROACHES

### Behavioral Programming

The first individual treatment method is that of behavioral programming. In a hospital setting, behavioral programming consists of the development of a learning theory based treatment program which is implemented on a unit-wide basis. All staff members are aware of the program and its procedures. Any programs that are restrictive or aversive must be approved by both administration plus a hospital-wide "Human Rights Committee." Various administrative guidelines must be followed, and data must be kept to determine program effectiveness. One means of reducing undesirable sexual behavior is to reward desirable behaviors. A credit incentive system is a highly effective method of encouraging appropriate behaviors in general (Liberman, Fearn, De Risi, Roberts, & Carmona, 1977). This is a system in which the client carries a card and is given points on it for desirable behaviors. These points may be used to obtain special activities or treats. Such a system also encourages the staff members to attend to desirable behavior while ignoring undesirable behavior. This is extremely important since attention to undesirable behavior can be reinforcing, whereas non-contingent attention does not make a clinical difference even if it is of a higher density than contingent attention (Paul & Lentz, 1977). Behavioral programs are highly effective with many problems in psychiatric populations and are used extensively with the developmentally disabled. Individualized behavioral programs may be used to treat sexual problems with the developmentally disabled. Differential reinforcement of other behavior (DRO) plus restitutional overcorrection have been used to eliminate inappropriate sexual behavior in a severely retarded person (Polivinale & Lutzker, 1980). Overcorrection has been used to effectively treat public disrobing in two profoundly retarded women (Foxx, 1976). Facial screening (contingent covering of the subject's face with a bib) has been effective in eliminating public masturbation in a severely retarded man (Barmann & Murray, 1981). Response cost has also been used to treat inappropriate sexual behavior (Schaefer & Martin, 1969). And DRO plus extinction were used to decrease public exposure in a profoundly retarded person (Lutzker, 1974).

A number of behavioral programs have been effective in treating sexual problems in dual diagnosis clients on the specialized unit. One example is the case of Jim, a 30-year-old man with an AAMD diagnosis of "mild mental retardation" with "hydrocephalus" and "psychotic behavior." Jim was very social and would frequently attempt to engage female staff members in conversations about touching their legs or about riding nude with them on a motorcycle. Usually he pursued new employees, students, or strangers, asking permission for what he wanted to do, or asking if their boyfriends or husbands would object. Initially, the staff provided Jim with information regarding the inappropriateness of such conversations and the possible consequences if this behavior was exhibited in the community. This was not effective, however. Since Jim loved to talk, a program was developed whereby the conversation with him would be immediately terminated whenever the topic became sexually inappropriate. In addition, every staff member would place Jim on social extinction by totally ignoring him for 15 minutes following this behavior. Jim was rather clever, however, and soon began approaching staff members to tell them how well he was doing on his new program. "I didn't talk to female staff members today about riding nude." Jim would then, of course, go into great detail to describe what things he had *not* talked about. The program needed to be revised so that any mention of various key words would lead to immediate termination of the conversation. This proved effective and, within three months, this behavior decreased from being a nearly daily event to occurring two times in six months and then zero times in six months.

Sandy was another dual diagnosis resident for whom behavioral programming was effective in treating a sexual problem. Using DSM-III criteria, her diagnosis was "histrionic personality disorder." Sandy exhibited frequent impulsive, attention-seeking behaviors, including suicidal gestures and threats, inappropriate touching of male staff members, dramatic fainting spells, fake seizures, exaggerated crying episodes, and frequent somatic complaints. Testing indicated a low suicidal intent and no significant depression. Treatment basically consisted of the staff ignoring her negative, attention-seeking behavior as long as it was not dangerous. Verbal praise, credit incentive points, and frequent, brief conversations were used when she behaved appropriately. Sandy's inappropriate attention-seeking behavior decreased from 98 times per month to 49, 51, 27, and 6 times per month consecutively. Inappropriate touching decreased in frequency from over 30 times per month to less than one occurrence per month. With the help of behavioral programming, Sandy was able to learn how to obtain attention by other more appropriate means. And a male staff member, who was harassed to the point of wanting to leave the unit, was greatly relieved.

## Individual Counseling

The second individual approach is that of counseling. Numerous authors have stated that counseling may be effective with developmentally disabled persons (Bialer, 1967; Gunzburg, 1974; Halpern & Bernard, 1974; Hayes, 1977; Jakab, 1970; Stamm, 1974; Stone & Coughlan, 1973). Unfortunately, very little controlled research has been conducted to evaluate the effectiveness of such counseling (Ingalls, 1978). Specific therapeutic techniques are rarely described (Dybuad, 1970). And very few studies ever obtain follow-up data to determine if the beneficial results of counseling are lasting.

Counseling with dual diagnosis clients can be either a brief, information-giving session or a more complex event. An example of a short-term, information-giving session was the time Ed approached me and stated rather abruptly, "I have a sex problem." When Ed was asked what this problem was, he declared, "I masturbate too much!" Further inquiry as to why this was a problem yielded some interesting information. Ed claimed that he masturbated several times per day because he was bored. "There's nothing else to do," he concluded. After a brief talk, we determined that it was okay to masturbate in private during free time. Masturbating was not really a problem for Ed. Boredom, however, was a problem, so we discussed possible ways to relieve some of the boredom and involved Ed in some leisure skills training. He soon reported that his "sex problem" was gone. And after two years it has not recurred.

Another brief counseling session also involved the issue of masturbation. John kept complaining to the unit physician about a recurring groin rash. He claimed that he developed the rash from masturbating. The unit physician wrote a physician's order for someone to counsel John regarding more appropriate ways of masturbating. Nursing staff members were incredulous. They were also embarrassed. The social worker, therefore, volunteered to do the counseling. I met with John for approximately 15 minutes. He felt comfortable discussing his masturbation, saying that he masturbated daily, that he did so while lying on his belly, and that the rashes occurred periodically. Postulating that the rash was due to friction with the bed sheets while lying face down, the suggestion was made to John that he try to masturbate while lying on his back. He agreed to do this, and the session ended. The next day John eagerly reported that he was able to successfully masturbate while lying on his back. Nearly a year has passed since then, and there have been no recurrences of the rash.

Not all counseling is so brief and simple, though. George was a 24-year-old, single man who was AAMD diagnosed as being mildly "mentally retarded with Down's syndrome" and "psychotic reaction." He was initially admitted to the hospital for physical aggression and property destruction. I had been counseling George on an in-patient basis for approximately six months. We met two to three times per week for 15 to 30 minutes. Primary focus was on George's depression which had been assessed from both clinical observation and testing and which was steadily improving.

Although George had shown a special interest in one of the women employees, he seemed to have little concern for sex. As his depression lifted, however, George's interest in sex gradually increased until it became obsessive and even delusional. George had a poor memory and was confused about his strong sexual feelings. It was probably hard for him to differentiate his feelings, thoughts and desires from his actual memory. In addition, George had always denied negative emotions and had often accused others of having feelings for him, such as anger, which were actually his feelings for them. He frequently talked about sex and even confronted numerous employees with complaints that they were "after his body." Finally, after one of his home visits, George came back claiming that his favorite female employee had come to his parents' house and had parked her car outside all night waiting for him. He knew her car license plate number and swore that he was able to identify it. This person had, in fact, been out of the country at the time. But George sincerely believed that he had seen her and the car.

Since a cognitive-behavioral approach had been useful in counseling George for his depression, I decided to utilize this approach with his current problem. Beck has suggested (1976) that emotional problems need not be rooted in the unconscious, but may instead result from difficulties in learning, from insufficient or incorrect information, or from confusions between imagination and reality. Because a direct attempt to convince George that he imagined everything would either alienate or upset him, I aligned myself with George by telling him that I knew he really believed that he saw the car. This calmed him down significantly. Before meticulously examining the basis for George's beliefs, I decided to place him in a paradoxical situation. "George," I told him, "some of the residents here are not too smart. Some of them are severely retarded and could not understand what we will be talking about. But you can. You are intelligent enough to be able to think and reason." George agreed that he was. I thereby appealed to his sense of wanting to be "normal," using it as a strength. George was, therefore, placed in a situation of either accepting the logical conclusion of our discussion or of admitting that he was not intelligent enough to reason.

George and I then carefully gathered all of the evidence. Since we were able to verify that the woman in question had been out of the country, we concluded that she could not have been outside his house at the same time. The idea that he had imagined everything was not acceptable to George. "Then maybe somebody who looked like her stole her car and came to my house," he suggested. We examined the probability of this and finally concluded that it was more likely that a similar car was in the street and that he didn't see the license plate clearly. Beck refers to this as "identifying the misconceptions, testing their validity and substituting more appropriate concepts" (Beck, 1976, p. 214). In a similar way we examined George's other beliefs, including the ones regarding his sexual concerns, chipping away not at George's perception of the situations but at his interpretations of them. We finally concluded that things are not always as they seem or as we wish they would be, and that strong desires sometimes contribute to the way we interpret events. After several days, George's sexual obsessions ceased, as did the related problems. Several years have passed and they have not recurred. Since many other variables were involved besides counseling, one cannot conclude that counseling was the effective variable.

However, it does seem to be a promising approach to use with the more intelligent and verbal clients.

Several weeks later, George came into my office, closed the door, and said that he had something important to tell me. "I've got to have a sex life!" he exclaimed. In exploring this with George, it became clear that he wanted a heterosexual friendship with a woman. Although George once had a girlfriend, he had never had sexual contact beyond kissing and holding hands. He was able to successfully masturbate but was no longer satisfied with this as his only source of sexual expression. After talking and role playing with George, it soon became apparent that he had little sexual knowledge and very few heterosocial skills. I decided to enroll George in our sex education class and to teach him heterosocial skills for initiating conversations and dating.

In George's case we had to start with some basics because he tended to talk almost exclusively about himself and to rarely listen to others. I worked with George on a daily basis both in my social skills training group and individually. His initial goals were to encourage others to talk about themselves and to listen to what they said. After six weeks, George began asking female residents out to lunch and out for coffee. We then began working on asking open-ended questions and on extending conversations. As George progressed, he became immensely pleased with his accomplishments and began reporting them regularly to us. Within three months George had a regular girlfriend.

## Social Skills Training

As many authors have observed, sexuality cannot be separated from social behavior (Gochros, 1972; Ullman & Krasner, 1975). Tollison (1979) indicates that lack of social skills for initiating relationships is a very common sexual problem. In an interview of institutionalized mentally disordered persons, the most frequently stated sexual problem was "no partner" (Wasow, 1980). One author advocates teaching social skills to disabled persons prior to sex therapy or group therapy (Gillman, 1980). Training in heterosocial skills has also been advocated as part of an overall group counseling approach for institutionalized mentally retarded persons (Zisfein & Rosen, 1973). The sex education instructor on the dual diagnosis unit reported that in attempting to be responsive to the residents' expressed concerns, the focus of the sex education class gradually shifted away from simple information giving toward discussion of interpersonal relationships.

Social skills training has been called "personal effectiveness training" (Liberman, King, De Risi, & McCann, 1975), "structured learning therapy" (Goldstein, 1973), as well as a variety of other names. The term social skills training is now generally considered the preferred term for the structured learning of abilities that form the basis of interpersonal communication. This may include the teaching of nonverbal, paralinguistic, cognitive, verbal, or problem-solving skills. Training may focus more on the learning of specific components of communication such as eye contact, hand gestures, facial expression, posture, voice volume, and so on. Or the sessions may place more emphasis on specific social situations such as handling anger, expressing affection, requesting help, or giving apologies. The training may also address the needs of specific groups of people, such as treating institutionalized persons how to function more effectively in the community (Goldstein, Sprafkin, & Gershaw, 1976) or helping adolescents within a school setting (Goldstein, Sprafkin, Gershaw, & Klein, 1980). Or it may be individualized to the psychological problems of an individual. One may want, for example, to teach a person with suicidal behavior how to appropriately obtain concern and interest from others. Or one might want to teach a depressed person how to be assertive and to make positive self-statements.

Although the general approach often varies with each trainer, there are certain components to social skills training that are considered basic. Social skills training may sometimes be taught on an individual basis, but group size usually varies between four and 15 persons. Either one scene is practiced by everyone in turn, or the scene is specific to each individual. The core of the training is *role playing* which is the acting out of brief scenes or problem situations. Verbal instructions, modeling, prompting, performance feedback, shaping, and reinforcement are often used in conjunction with the role playing. Once the skill is learned or acquired, homework assignments and other techniques are used to encourage generalization and overlearning. After a behavior generalizes to other places and situations, the natural reinforcers in the environment help to maintain the behavior. Acquisition, generalization, and maintenance are the stages whereby a social skill becomes a part of a person's behavioral repertoire.

Although there has not been any published research regarding the effectiveness of social skills training with dual diagnosis persons, there has been some research with chronic psychiatric residents who were also diagnosed as mentally retarded (presumably, the mental retardation was a result of the chronic mental disorder). Two studies addressed argumentative and physically assaultive behavior (Matson & Stevens, 1978; Matson & Zeiss, 1978). In another experiment with a similar population, social skills training was significantly more effective than contingent reinforcement in 15 different behavior areas (Matson, Zeiss, Zeiss, & Bowman, 1980). There is also considerable research indicating that social skills training is effective with mentally retarded persons (Bates, 1980; Bornstein, Bach, McFall, Friman, & Lyons, 1980; Gibson, Lawrence, & Nelson, 1976: Matson, 1978; Nelson, Gibson, & Cutting, 1973; Ross, 1969; Senatore, Matson, & Kazdin, 1982; Turner, Hersen, & Bellack, 1978; Whitman, Mercurio, & Caponigri, 1970). And social skills training appears to be significantly more effective than traditional psychotherapy (Matson & Senatore, 1981).

The area of social skills training that is particularly relevant to sexuality is the area of *heterosocial skills*. Heterosocial skills are the skills related to the initiation, development, and maintenance of social and possibly sexual relationships with persons of the other sex. Treatment generally focuses on decreasing heterosocial anxiety or on teaching specific heterosocial skills. Treatment for heterosocial anxiety may include systematic desensitization, cognitive approaches, or various combinations of practice and reinforcement. Teaching heterosocial skills often includes social skills training in such areas as asking open-ended questions, extending conversations, disclosing self-information, having appropriate physical appearance, and being pleasant or reinforcing (Tollison & Adams, 1979). Unfortunately, much of the research involving heterosocial skills uses college students (Galassi & Galassi, 1979; Tollison & Adams, 1979). Many of the specific skills and teaching techniques may therefore have to be modified for dual diagnosis persons.

In dealing with heterosocial difficulties with dual diagnosis clients, I conduct social skills training which emphasizes response acquisition. This assumes that the residents have an actual skills deficit as opposed to simply a need to practice (response practice) or a need to encourage interaction (self-reinforcement). The actual training is a combination of several approaches but is based mostly on

Liberman's "personal effectiveness training" (Liberman et al., 1975). Liberman's approach is admirably simple, yet highly effective. My social skills groups are each composed of from four to six residents. A group session lasts about 30 minutes. Initially, groups were composed of 10 or more residents, had three to six therapists, and ran for one hour. It was found, however, that smaller, shorter duration groups could be more homogenous, could more easily maintain the attention of the residents, and could even be conducted by one therapist alone.

Since most of the residents wish to leave the hospital, the sessions center around learning the skills that are necessary during community placement. Unlike most social skills training groups, every session begins with a short group discussion which actively engages each resident. This preliminary discussion encourages all of the residents to be involved and demonstrates the relevance of the upcoming scene. If the session, for example, was to be on "giving compliments," then the initial discussion would use active directive teaching and problem solving to point out the value of giving compliments and its relevance to being in the community.

The next step is for each resident to role play a similar scene at the session while working on specific deficit areas. All residents, for example, might take turns pretending that they had been discharged to a residential care home where they met someone with whom they wanted to make friends. They would role play "making introductions" or "giving compliments." One resident would be asked to be the "new person" while each of the other residents would be given an assignment to observe for certain behaviors such as eye contact, voice volume, and so on, depending on what deficit areas the practicing individual was working on. A dry run is generally conducted first, followed by constructive feedback from the other residents and the therapist. Through verbal prompts and positive interpretations by the therapist, feedback by others is kept positive and reinforcing. Likewise, feedback from the therapist is always supportive and encouraging, focusing on what the client did well, while briefly mentioning a few suggestions on how the role play could be even better. This is then followed by a second role play during which modeling, hand gestures, verbal prompts, or other techniques may be utilized by the therapist as needed. Positive feedback is given again, and the role play ends with a round of applause and a homework assignment.

The effectiveness of this training is evaluated on a single case basis. A one-month baseline is taken using direct behavioral observations during probes. Monthly data are then kept and graphed for each resident. When an objective is met, a new objective or skill is designated. Very positive results have so far been obtained. Research needs to be conducted with dual diagnosis clients in several areas. These include: (a) developing a reliable means to assess their heterosocial skills and deficits, (b) evaluating and comparing various individual and group treatment approaches to increase heterosocial skills, (c) determining the effective components of social skills training, (d) comparing heterosocial skills in dual diagnosis persons with comparable groups of mentally disordered and developmentally disabled persons, and (e) developing techniques to encourage generalization and maintenance of skills.

## Sex Education

Sex education is the other group approach utilized for the treatment of sexual problems and concerns of dual diagnosis clients. Although there is no literature in the area of sex education for dual diagnosis persons, there is a vast amount of literature regarding sex education for the developmentally disabled. Sexual knowledge may be acquired by moderately and severely retarded individuals (Edmonson, McCombs, & Wish, 1979). Sex education for the developmentally disabled is a need which has received widespread recognition (Edmonson & Wish, 1975; Johnson, 1973). Developmentally disabled persons often do not have opportunities to learn through other educational and social channels (Kempton, 1978). Hall (1974) notes that many studies indicate that sex education is desirable, that what is needed are more specific ways to teach it and to measure its effectiveness.

The sex education class for dual diagnosis clients is called "personal awareness education." The areas covered include: (a) anatomy (identification and function), (b) emotional/social (self-concept, kinds of love, interaction skills, appropriate versus inappropriate behaviors), (c) precautions (birth control and diseases), (d) legal (laws regarding sexual behavior). Films, mannikin models, pamphlets, and various visual aids are utilized. Role playing and group discussions are helpful. The means of measurement used are multiple choice pre- and posttests. Although all of the residents have taken the course, a few of them have been referred to the class because of special sexual problems. Joseph was one of these residents who was referred.

Another resident reported that Joseph had worn a condom all night while asleep. When asked about this, Joseph replied, "Well, I heard you should wear one of these if you've been having sex." Joseph was subsequently enrolled in the sex education class. After taking the pretest and scoring 11 correct out of 50, Joseph participated in four months of classes, meeting for three hours twice per week. During the sessions, many of Joseph's questions and concerns were addressed. His posttest score was 46 out of 50, an increase of 35 points. Afterwards, Joseph could carefully explain the correct need and use of a condom.

Sex education may also occur informally. One dual diagnosis resident, Paul, was sitting in the common area of one of the dorms. As I walked past him, he fidgeted quickly. After passing by a few minutes later, I realized that Paul was masturbating and that he quickly covered up his penis whenever anyone went by. Because Paul was in a public area and several other residents were present, I asked him if he would please go to his bed to masturbate. It was explained that it was not appropriate to masturbate in a public place because this upset some people. It was okay, he was told, to masturbate during free time if it was done under the covers of one's bed. Paul then went to his bed and continued to masturbate. Since Paul covered himself both times that I passed by, it seemed probable that he knew he was being socially inappropriate. After talking to him later, I learned that this was indeed the case. Paul did not, however, know that it was okay to go to his bed during the daytime because sleeping during the daytime was strongly discouraged by staff. He thought that if he went to his bed someone would tell him to get up, and he felt too embarrassed to explain that he was in bed to masturbate rather than to sleep. Afterwards, I talked to some of the unit staff members, explaining the situation to them. They agreed to give Paul some free time in bed each day.

As can be seen in the last case example, it is often difficult to separate the clinical issues of sexuality from the social and institutional ones. Some authors, in fact, claim that sex education for clients need not be overly involved and that what is needed most is a change in the attitudes of those people who work with the handicapped (Gordon, Note 2). Others point out the need in hospitals for more staff discussion regarding sexual issues (Wolfe & Menninger, 1973). Behavioral rehearsal has been advocated as part of a continuing education program for nursing staff in order to help them to be more comfortable in discussing sexual matters with their patients (Withersity, 1976). Educational workshops for professionals and paraprofessionals appear to be effective in increasing their acceptance of sexual expression in developmentally disabled persons (Hall, 1978). Other authors advocate educating society in general so that developmentally disabled persons can be accepted as sexual beings (Friedman, 1971; Morgenstern, 1973). Promoting humane attitudes and social policies toward sexual behavior is seen by one author as a primary task for social workers (Kirk, 1977). Sex education, then, can mean educating our clients, or those who work with them, or society in general.

Although this article has been concerned with the clinical treatment of sexual problems, it should be emphasized very strongly that there are other sexual problems for dual diagnosis persons that are extremely important. Personal sexual issues cannot be separated from society or its various regulations and infringements. Social workers and other professionals must be equally concerned with the oppressive social and institutional forces that control and shape the sexual lives of our clients. Only then will clinical problems be addressed in their true entirety.

## REFERENCE NOTES

1. Perske, R. *Mental retardation: The leading edge, programs that work.* Washington, D.C.: U.S. Government Printing Office, 1979.
2. Gordon, S. *Sex education for neglected youth: Retarded, handicapped, emotionally disturbed and learning disabled.* Santa Barbara, California, Planned Parenthood, 1975.

## REFERENCES

Andreasen, N. C. Sexual problems and affective disorders. *Medical Aspects of Human Sexuality,* 1981, *15,* 134-143.
Barmann, B. C., & Murray, W. J. Suppression of inappropriate sexual behavior by facial screening. *Behavior Therapy,* 1981, *12,* 730-735.
Bates, P. The effectiveness of interpersonal skills training on the social skill acquisition of moderately and mildly retarded adults. *Journal of Applied Behavior Analysis,* 1980, *13,* 237-248.
Beck, A. T. Sexuality and depression. *Medical Aspects of Human Sexuality,* 1968, *2,* 44-51.
Beck, A. T. *Cognitive therapy and emotional disorders.* New York: International Universities Press, 1976.
Bialer, I. Psychotherapy and other adjustment techniques with the mentally retarded. In A. Baumeister (Ed.), *Mental retardation: Appraisal, education, and rehabilitation.* Hawthorne, New York: Aldine, 1967.

Bornstein, P., Bach, P. J., McFall, M. E., Friman, P. C., & Lyons, P. D. Application of a social skills training program in the modification of interpersonal deficits among retarded adults: A clinical replication. *Journal of Applied Behavior Analysis,* 1980, *13,* 171-176.

Committee on Mental Retardation, Psychiatric consultations in mental retardation. *Group for the Advancement of Psychiatry,* 1979, *10,* 598-692.

Dybuad, G. Psychiatry's role in mental retardation. In N. Bernstein (Ed.), *Diminished people: Problems of the mentally retarded.* Boston: Little, Brown & Co., 1970.

Edmonson, B., McCombs, K., & Wish, J. What retarded adults believe about sex. *American Journal of Mental Deficiency,* 1979, *84,* 11-18.

Edmonson, B., & Wish, J. Sex knowledge and attitudes of moderately retarded males. *American Journal of Mental Deficiency,* 1975, *80,* 172-179.

Foxx, R. M. The use of overcorrection to eliminate the public disrobing (stripping) of retarded women. *Behaviour Research and Therapy.* 1976, *14,* 53-60.

Friedman, E. Missing in the life of the retarded individual—sex: Reflections on Sol Gordon's paper. *Journal of Special Education,* 1971, *5,* 365-368.

Galassi, J. P., & Galassi, M. D. Modification of heterosocial skills deficits. In A. S. Bellack & M. Herson (Eds.), *Research to practice in social skills training.* New York: Plenum Press, 1979.

Gerner, R. H. Hypersexuality of manics. *Medical Aspects of Human Sexuality,* 1981, *15,* 99.

Gibson, F. W., Jr., Lawrence, P. S., & Nelson, R. O. Comparison of three training procedures for teaching social responses to developmentally disabled adults. *American Journal of Mental Deficiency,* 1976, *81,* 379-387.

Gillan, P. Psychological methods in sex therapy for the disabled. *Sexuality and Disability,* 1980, *3,* 199-202.

Gochros, H. L. Social work's sexual blinders. In H. L. Gochros & L. G. Schultz (Eds.), *Human sexuality and social work.* New York: Association Press, 1972.

Goldstein, A. P. *Structured learning therapy: Toward a psychotherapy for the poor.* New York: Academic Press, 1973.

Goldstein, A. P., Sprafkin, R. P., Gershaw, N. J., & Klein, P. *Skill streaming the adolescent: A structured learning approach to teaching prosocial skills.* Champaign, Illinois: Research Press, 1980.

Goldstein, A. P., Sprafkin, R. P., & Genshaw, N. J. *Skill training for community living: Applying structured learning therapy.* New York: Pergamon Press, 1976.

Gualtieri, C. Thomas. Psychiatry's disinterest in mental retardation. *Psychiatric Opinion,* May 1979, 26-28.

Gunzburg, H. C. Psyhchotherapy with the feeble-minded. In A. M. Clarke & A.D.B. Clarkey (Eds.), *Mental deficiency* (Vol. 11). New York: Free Press, 1974.

Hall, J. E. Sexual behavior. In J. Wortis (Ed.), *Mental retardation and developmental disabilities: An annual review VI.* New York: Brunner/Mazel, 1974.

Hall, J. E. Acceptance of sexual expression in the mentally retarded. *Sexuality and Disability,* 1978, *1,* 44-51.

Halpern, A. S., & Berard, W. R. Counseling the mentally retarded: A review for practice. In P. L. Browning (Ed.), *Mental retardation: Rehabilitation and counseling.* Springfield, Illinois: Charles C. Thomas, 1974.

Hayes, M. The responsiveness of mentally retarded children to psychotherapy. *Smith College Studies in Social Work,* 1977, *47,* 112-153.

Heaton-Ward, A. Psychosis in mental handicap. *British Journal of Psychiatry,* 1977, *130,* 525-533.

Hersh, A., & Brown, G. Preparation of mental health personnel for the delivery of mental retardation services. *Community Mental Health Journal,* 1977, *13,* 13-23.

Ingalls, R.P. Treatment of behavioral and emotional problems. In F.P. Ingalls (Ed.), *Mental retardation: The changing outlook.* New York: John Wiley & Sons, 1978.

Jakab, I. Psychotherapy of the mentally retarded child. In N. R. Bernstein (Ed.), *Diminished people: Problems and care of the mentally retarded.* Boston: Little, Brown & Co., 1970.

Johnson, W. R. Sex education of the mentally retarded. In F. F. De La Cruz & G. D. La

Veck (Eds.), *Human sexuality and the mentally retarded.* New York: Brunner/Mazel, 1973.

Kempton, W. Sex education for the mentally handicapped. *Sexuality and Disability,* 1978, *1,* 137-145.

Kirk, S. A. Society and sexual deviance. In H. L. Gochros & J. S. Gochros (Eds.), *The sexually oppressed.* New York: Association Press, 1977.

Liberman, R. P., Fearn, C. H., De Risi, W., Roberts, J., & Carmona, M. The credit-incentive system: Motivating the participation of patients in a day hospital. *British Journal of Social and Clinical Psychology,* 1977, *16,* 85-94.

Liberman, R. P., King, L. W., De Risi, W. J., & McCann, M. *Personal effectiveness: Guiding people to assert themselves and improve their social skills.* Champaign, Illinois: Research Press, 1975.

Lutzker, J. R. Social reinforcement control of exhibitionism in a profoundly retarded adult. *Mental Retardation,* 1974, *12,* 46-47.

Mandelbaum, A. Mental health and retardation. In J. B. Turner (Ed.), *Encyclopedia of Social Work* (Vol. 2). Washington, D. C.: National Association of Social Workers, 1977.

Marks, I. M. Management of sexual disorders. In H. Leitenberg (Ed.), *Handbook of behavior modification and behavior therapy.* Englewood Cliffs, New Jersey: Prentice-Hall, 1976.

Matson, J. L. Training socially appropriate behaviors to moderately retarded adults with contingent praise, instructions, feedback and a modified self-recording procedure. *Scandanavian Journal of Behavior Therapy,* 1978, *7,* 167-175.

Matson, J. L., & Senatore, V. A comparison of traditional psychotherapy and social skills training for improving interpersonal functioning of mentally retarded adults. *Behavior Therapy,* 1981, *12,* 369-382.

Matson, J. L., & Stephens, R. M. Increasing appropriate behavior of explosive chronic psychiatric patients with a social skills training package. *Behavior Modification,* 1978, *2,* 61-65.

Matson, J. L., & Zeiss, R. A. Group training of social skills in chronically explosive, severely disturbed psychiatric patients. *Behavior Engineering,* 1978, *5,* 41-51.

Matson, J. L., Zeiss, R. A., Zeiss, T., & Bowman, W. A. A comparison of social skills training and contingent attention to improve behavioral deficits of chronic psychiatric patients. *British Journal of Social and Clinical Psychology,* 1980, *19,* 57-64.

Menolascino, F. J. Emotional disturbance and mental retardation. *American Journal of Mental Deficiency,* 1965, *70,* 248-256.

Menolascino, F. J. The facade of mental retardation: Its challenge to child psychiatry. *American Journal of Psychiatry,* 1966, *122,* 1227-1235.

Menolascino, F. J. The research challenge of delineating psychiatric syndromes in mental retardation. In F. J. Menolascino (Ed.), *Psychiatric Approaches to Mental Retardation.* New York: Basic Books, 1970.

Morganstern, M. Community attitudes toward sexuality of the retarded. In F. F. De La Cruz & G. D. La Veck (Eds.), *Human sexuality and the mentally retarded.* New York: Brunner/Mazel, 1973.

Nelson, R., Gibson, F., Jr., & Cutting, D. S. Video taped modeling: The development of three appropriate social responses in a mildly retarded child. *Mental Retardation,* 1973, *11,* 24-28.

Paul, G. L., & Lentz, R. J. *Psychosocial treatment of chronic mental patients: Milieu versus social-learning programs.* Cambridge, Massachusetts: Harvard University Press, 1977.

Philips, I. Psychopathology and mental retardation. *American Journal of Psychiatry,* 1967, *124,* 29-35.

Philips, I., & Williams, N. Psychopathology and mental retardation: A study of 100 mentally retarded children: 1. Psychopathology. *American Journal of Psychiatry,* 1975, *132,* 1265-1271.

Pinderhughes, C. A., Grace, E. B., & Reyna, J. Psychiatric disorders and sexual functioning. *American Journal of Psychiatry,* 1972, *128,* 1276-1283.

Polivindale, R. A., & Lutzker, J. R. Elimination of assaultive and inappropriate sexual behavior by reinforcement and social restitution. *Mental Retardation*, 1980, *18*, 27-30.

Potter, H. Mental retardation: The Cinderella of psychiatry. *Psychiatric Quarterly*, 1965, *39*, 537-549.

Ross, S. A. Effects of intentional training in social behavior on retarded children. *American Journal of Mental Deficiency*, 1969, *73*, 912-919.

Sarino, M. R., Sterns, E. M., & Kennedy, R. The lack of services to the retarded through community mental health programs. *Community Mental Health Journal*, 1973, *9*, 158-168.

Scalon, P. L. Social work with the mentally retarded client. *Social Casework*, 1978, *59*, 161-166.

Schaefer, H. H., & Martin, P. L. *Behavior Therapy*. New York: McGraw-Hill, 1969.

Selan, V. A. Psychotherapy with the developmentally disabled. *Health and Social Work*, 1976, *1*, 73-85.

Senatore, V., Matson, J. L., & Kazdin, A. E. A comparison of behavioral methods to train social skills to mentally retarded adults. *Behavior Therapy*, 1982, *13*, 313-324.

Stamm, J. Behavioral counseling with the mentally retarded. In P. L. Browning (Ed.), *Mental retardation: Rehabilitation and counseling*. Springfield, Illinois: Charles C Thomas, 1974.

Sha'Ked, A. *Human sexuality in physical and mental illness and disabilities*. Bloomington, Indiana: Indiana University Press, 1978.

Small, I. F., & Small, J. G. Sexual behavior and mental illness. In B. J. Sadock, H. I. Kaplan, & A. M. Freedman (Eds.), *The Sexual Experience*. Baltimore: Williams & Williams Co., 1976.

Stone, S., & Coughlan, P. Four process variables in counseling with mentally retarded clients. *American Journal of Mental Deficiency*, 1973, *11*, 408-414.

Tollison, C. D., & Adams, H. E. *Sexual disorders: Treatment, theory, and research*. New York: Gardner Press, 1979.

Tsuang, M. T. Hypersexuality in manic patients. *Medical Aspects of Human Sexuality*, 1975, *9*, 83-89.

Turner, S. M., Hersen, M., & Bellack, A. S. Use of social skills training to teach prosocial behaviors in an organically impaired and retarded patient. *Journal of Behavior Therapy and Experimental Psychiatry*, 1978, *9*, 253-258.

Ullman, L. P., & Drasner, L. *A psychological approach to abnormal behavior*. Englewood Cliffs, New Jersey: Prentice-Hall, 1975.

Walker, P. Recognizing the mental health needs of developmentally disabled people. *Social Casework*, 1980, *25*, 293-297.

Wasow, M. Sexuality and the institutionalized mentally ill. *Sexuality and Disability*, 1980, *3*, 3-16.

Webster, T. Problems of emotional development in young retarded children. *American Journal of Psychiatry*, 1963, *120*, 37-43.

Whitman, T. L., Mercurio, J. R., & Caponigri, V. Development of social responses in two severely retarded children. *Journal of Applied Behavior Analysis*, 1970, *3*, 133-138.

Winokur, B. Subnormality and its relation to psychiatry. *Lancet*, 1974, *2*, 270-272.

Winokur, G., Clayton, P. J., & Reich, T. *Manic depressive illness*. St. Louis: Mosby, 1969.

Withersity, D. J. Sexual attitudes of hospital personnel: A model for continuing education. *American Journal of Psychiatry*, 1976, *5*, 573-575.

Wolfe, S. D., & Menninger, W. W. Fostering open communication about sexual concerns in a mental hospital. *Hospital and Community Psychiatry*, 1973, *24*, 147-150.

Zisfein, L., & Rosen, M. Personal adjustment training: A group counseling program for institutionalized mentally retarded persons. *Mental Retardation*, 1973, *11*, 16-20.